DOUBLE YOUR SALARY

Without losing your soul

MARK ANDERSON SMITH

To Davina

Merry Christmas

Mark

2019

First published in Great Britain in 2019 by
Dragon Lake Books
An imprint of Mark Anderson Smith

www.dragonlake.co.uk
books@dragonlake.co.uk

A catalogue record for this book is available
from the British Library.

ISBN: 978-0-9929883-9-5

To Nelson and Mary

You taught me the importance of hard work
and what really matters in life.

Thank you!

Books by Mark Anderson Smith

The Great Scottish Land Grab

Fallen Warriors

Contents

Introduction

Why double your salary

I've always wanted to be able to provide for my family. It never occurred to me that I might not be able to do that. When our first child was born, my wife earned more money than I did. It made sense that she would return to work after maternity leave and I would take on the role of house-husband. I didn't have a trade, had never been to college or university, I'd been working at whatever job I could pick up and had to take whatever salary or wage was offered.

For the next year I looked after my daughter and it seemed like one long extended holiday. Then our circumstances changed. A few years later we had two children, my wife was now struggling to get a job that paid well, and I had come to realise that I needed to work.

I'd begun to understand that I have a deep need for meaningful work, and that my self-esteem is tied up in my ability to provide for my family. That extended holiday had unsettled me, made me question who I was, what value I had.

Everyone needs to double their salary at least once every twenty five years. If you don't then inflation will have robbed you of the value of your earnings and you'll be poorer than you were. In reality, inflation probably robs you faster than that. If you look at minimum wage today compared to similar wages two and a half decades ago, then you would have had to double your salary twice in that time just to keep up!

I didn't set out then to double my salary, but knew I needed to earn more. I focussed on developing a career and within a year started to earn a wage better than I'd ever had. Within four years I'd doubled my salary only to find it wasn't enough…

By that time we had three children, two of whom were now in primary school. If you've got children, or even remember from your own childhood, they tend to go through clothes fast. They fall and skin their knees, tearing a hole in trousers or tights. They drag their feet while they walk, scuffing their shoes or trainers, kicking at stones, not realising that the more they damage their shoes the more frequently they need replaced.

Well, our children needed new shoes. I think possibly all of them did, three pairs, a bill bomb that we hadn't budgeted for, hadn't saved for and couldn't afford.

Not that we weren't trying to budget and save, we were. A year or so before, I'd been offered a permanent job earning more money than I'd ever earned. Yet the bills kept coming in: new car exhaust, replacement car tyres, school clothes, council tax increases… How could I be earning so much money and yet it still wasn't enough?

Even the government was giving us money. At the time we were receiving Tax Credits, a kind of benefit that topped up our income because one of us was working but not earning enough. Yes, I'd doubled my salary, but even so, the government still believed we weren't earning enough.

Something just didn't add up.

One morning I was sitting in our kitchen, trying to work out how we were going to pay for these new shoes when I heard something being pushed through our letter box. A plain white envelope with no writing on the front, but inside was £100. Someone, I suspect from our church, had kindly given us a gift.

I was brought to tears. I have to say mostly from shame, shame that I wasn't able to provide for our family, shame that we had to rely on charity and government benefits. But also I was grateful that someone saw that we were in need and did something to help.

We bought our children new shoes. I kept thinking. I didn't want to remain poor. I believed that it must be possible to do something about it. However, I didn't know how or what I needed to do. As you read on, you'll find that for most of my working life I've not had a plan. From one perspective you could argue that I've stumbled from one opportunity to another. I didn't set out to double my salary, and yet when I did make that my goal, I realised I'd already done just that a couple of times before.

I started analysing what had happened, trying to learn from decisions I'd made, from the situations I found myself in. I found there were patterns that emerged, underlying reasons why I was successful in some situations and why I failed in others. I began to wonder if what I was learning about myself could be helpful to others. Maybe even to you.

My hope with this book is that it will inspire you to question a worldview that things cannot change. I share my struggles, my doubts, the questions I asked, the risks I took, the dreams and visions I had, and what I did that ultimately enabled me to achieve my goal. Your life can change.

Change is scary for many people. Change is not always good and yet change is the only way things can get better.

Whether you realise it or not, you have skills, talents and gifts that you can use to earn more money. You also have the ability to learn additional skills and talents, to gain new knowledge that will help you, if you choose.

This book is not a plan for your life. You are different to me even though some of our experience may have been similar. I've worked on a production line many times. I've been a shop assistant, worked in a laundry, driven forklifts, loaded baggage in the pouring rain, worked behind the scenes in a store and have even changed the nappies of incontinent patients. I know what it's like to walk home tired with my back aching and my hands raw.

You may share some of my skills and abilities, but it is likely you have skills I do not possess, talents and gifts that I cannot use. Your experience will be different, your education, your knowledge and what you have may enable you to succeed where I have failed, or even to achieve more than I have done. I cannot give you a map for what you should do if you want to double your salary.

However, I believe that I've benefited from some universal truths, principles that will enable anyone to succeed in life. This book is focused on doubling your salary, but as I've shared it with trusted friends, their feedback has been that much of what I share is applicable in other parts of life: in relationships, in health, even in sport. Whoever you are, wherever you are in the world, regardless of what you currently earn, you can double your salary or at the very least improve your circumstances.

I'm very aware though that the pursuit of wealth is not going to lead anyone to happiness. How many times have you heard stories of the rich on their death beds recognising that family and friends should have been more important. I've sub-titled this book: without losing your soul. Jesus was quoted as saying no-one can serve both God and money. Having achieved my goal to double my salary, I'm very conscious of the sacrifices my family had to make. Time was the biggest sacrifice, time when I was locked away studying or staying late at work. Stress was another cost when the weight of what sometimes seemed an impossible task became too much. It is likely there will be a cost to pursuing the goal of doubling your salary, I do not want to hide that from you.

Given these risks, is it worth attempting to double your salary?

- Being able to provide for our family will reduce our stress and will satisfy one of our deepest needs.
- If we are appropriately rewarded for our effort, this will increase our contentment. It is tremendously

satisfying to work hard and then receive a justified reward.

- If we are capable of achieving more, if we aim to reach our full potential, this will not only benefit us, but benefit those around us, even our society.
- Earning more will allow us to free ourselves from debt.

In setting out to double your salary, you will have to question who you really are, what drives you, why you do what you do. What is your purpose in life? What are your skills and talents? Answering these questions may take years. You may even find the journey proves more valuable than the destination. It has for me.

I've split this book into six sections. I share the three goals that changed my life, then share my story, from my first job to the point where I doubled my salary a third time. Finally I end with a series of short chapters that focus on a particular topic. I share my experience, my beliefs, my theories and knowledge in the hope that all this will help you on your journey. I believe you are capable of transforming your life. May this book help you on your way.

The Three Goals That Changed My Life

Three goals

Have you ever had a dream? Some childhood ambition or wish or aspiration that you've never fulfilled? Mine was to be a writer. Specifically, I wanted to create worlds and tell stories set in those worlds, and when I say worlds, I mean worlds. I consumed every science fiction book I could find in our home library in Lerwick, Shetland.

Childhood dreams can get knocked out of you pretty early on. Growing up in the UK education system it didn't take me all that long to realise that my teachers didn't think writing was a career worth pursuing. It wasn't much different outside of school. When I gave my answer to the question: what do you want to do when you grow up, I learned that telling people I wanted to be an architect got a far better response.

I never really wanted to be an architect. I certainly wasn't prepared to commit to seven years of hard study after leaving school.

What do you want to do with your life? Who do you want to be? Do those questions seem odd in a book that proposes you can double your salary? I believe they are vital to ask.

In 2007 I wrote down three goals. I didn't realise the extent of it at the time, but they each said something very important about me as a person—who I was and who I wanted to be. Here were my three goals:

1) I will double my salary to £40,000
2) I will complete a university degree
3) I will write a novel

I added the following condition: I will achieve all these goals by the time I am forty.

I was about to turn 36.

At the time I wrote those three goals down, I wasn't sure if I would be able to complete them. I knew I was setting myself an impossible task. Yet, as I was to find, impossible only means you haven't done that yet.

I wrote the goals down in secret, without fanfare or announcement. Eventually though, I told my wife…

She wasn't impressed.

She had completed her university degree ten years before, studying full time, and knew how difficult it would be to do part time. She wisely advised that picking one goal and focusing on that would be far more achievable.

There are times when I'm not very good at listening to wise advice.

Deep down, I knew these goals were important to me. They each said something about who I wanted to be and I wasn't prepared to let any of them go.

Writing a novel was possibly the least important of the three, at least in terms of how it would change our lives. Yet it was also the most important to me personally. For almost thirty years I'd wanted to be a writer. I'd written a dozen short stories and jotted down dozens more ideas. I'd even had a few articles published some years previously, though hadn't continued to pursue that.

I was working on a novel, one that I'd started that year. It would take almost ten years before I finally completed and published that novel, but I knew that to be true to myself, I had to make an effort to pursue my dream.

For me, in the career path I'd chosen, seeking to earn a university degree was a sensible ambition. For other careers, certification or training courses can have similar benefits.

In Computing related job adverts, higher paid roles often cite a degree as one of the criteria for applications, others look for specific training qualifications. If you did not head straight to university or college after school, then returning to further education as an adult, or making the effort to gain additional training, shows a drive and commitment that many employers value. Continuous self-education is something looked for in many higher paid roles. It is a sign of a professional that you make an effort to keep abreast of new techniques and methods, that you see it as your responsibility to train yourself to learn additional skills.

Granted, you've no doubt heard of the thousands who graduate from university and college struggling even to find a job in a fast food outlet, yet training and university education can open doors that might otherwise have been closed.

I had seen first-hand how, even before I gained a college certificate, the mere fact I was on a college course (a Higher National Certificate in Computing) allowed me to secure my first IT contract. I'd noticed that some job descriptions mentioned 'degree' as a criterion and could see how I would expand the possibilities by going on to complete a degree course.

I ended up taking a tentative route towards my degree. As I needed to keep working, I signed up to the Open University's distance learning and took one course at a time. I focused initially on software development courses that were related to my new career in computing. This allowed me to extend my CV, but more importantly, proved useful in a key contract I ended up gaining a couple of years later.

In the summer of 2008, I received a phone call, while on a train in Paris… I'd been left a small inheritance and we'd decided to use it on a 'once in a lifetime' family holiday to Disneyland Paris. The phone call was from an agency looking for someone to take on a six-month contract paying £190 a day. Was I interested? I did some back of an envelope calculations and worked out that if I worked for six months, I'd almost earn my £23,000 annual salary in that time. If the contract was extended to a year…

I said I was interested.

I look back on those three goals and believe that they were instrumental in changing my life. There was a synchronicity between them. As I practised the art of writing, I was able to use that towards my degree. As I gained skills in research, I was able to apply that to my work and to my writing. As I began to earn more, I was able to afford additional further education courses. I was also able to buy the tools I needed as a writer, a new laptop and software.

Working towards each goal made the other goals easier to achieve, but it wasn't all going to be plain sailing!

Some strange beliefs

Companies that I've worked for in the UK are very similar in a lot of ways. Over the years I've frequently found my own beliefs at odds with the prevalent culture within the companies I've worked for.

Here are a few of my strange beliefs:

I believe that all employees should be paid a living wage for doing a basic job.

Over the last decade there has been a greater recognition that those who work should receive at the very least, not just a minimum wage, but a living wage. I've been very influenced by the work of the Joseph Rowntree Foundation in researching this. To pay anyone less than a living wage for doing a day's work is to trap them in poverty.

I believe that employees who go beyond their basic role should be rewarded for doing so.

It simply seems common sense to me that employees should be rewarded for doing more than is expected. If we are not slaves, then why would we sacrifice our time and energy for no reward? Every employee should be given clear guidelines for what is expected as part of their normal job. If an employee, of their own free will, wants to do more, this benefits the company, why should they not share in any profit the company makes as a result?

I believe that rewards for better, faster, more intelligent work should not depend on any other team member or department.

Also, I see no logical reason why any reward I receive should depend on someone else, or be held back because someone else failed to do their job. Some organisations implement policies around rewards that tie bonuses to the performance of a team, rather than an individual. I've seen individuals lose out on a bonus, or had their bonus reduced because others in a team were unable or unwilling to match the effort they had put in. There may be a short-term benefit to an organisation to reduce a bonus in such a scenario, but in the long term, for how long will that employee continue to put in the same amount of effort? My observation is that the morale of an entire team can be undercut because of one or two individuals who hold back the performance of the whole team.

I believe that in Britain we under pay and under value far too many employees.

A few years ago, I started researching salaries, income and profits made by companies. I was horrified to find that at the peak, some company directors were receiving over 300 times more in salary and bonus than the lowest paid members of their companies. When you consider that historically, company owners have only received 25 to 30 times as much as their lowest paid employees, it is hard to imagine how these directors can justify such high levels of pay and bonus. Every well-run company depends on employees at all levels to provide goods and services, to manage operations, and to interact with customers. Without employees you are just a one-man band, and while some individuals can do incredibly great things on their own, the moment you entrust someone else to work for you, you are both allowing and enabling them to help you make more money. Companies do not earn vast profits because they have a stellar executive team; they earn vast profits because thousands of employees satisfy millions of customers, deal with countless thousands of problems, and keep the company functioning. For a company director to even think that only their effort deserves to receive the highest reward is an injustice.

I believe that I should be able to earn at least £1,000 per year for every year I've been alive…

This belief is a little harder to justify, especially given its history…

By the time I was eighteen, I was on my second "permanent" job, earning £13,000 a year. Back in 1990, this was a decent income for an eighteen-year-old and I knew I was earning a good income.

Even back then, I was struggling to understand how the world worked in regard to salaries and incomes. There didn't seem to be much logic, with some people that I regarded highly, apparently only just scraping by, others who seemed to do no work of value were earning a lot.

I've always wanted to believe there is order to the world, but in the absence of a logical pattern, I decided to invent my own. It seemed reasonable to me that anyone who continued to gain knowledge and experience would become more valuable to employers as time passed. If I consistently applied myself to learning and training, I should be able to justify that I also would consistently gain a higher income.

But how much could I expect to gain on a regular basis? I had the option to take my current income as a starting point—£13,000. If that was what I was worth, then perhaps I could divide that by 18 and then use that value to state what each year of my experience was worth. Then plan that I should see an equivalent increase year on year.

£13,000 divided by 18… Some people excel at that sort of mental arithmetic, I have to work at it! Interestingly, when you are just playing around with numbers, it often makes sense to simplify. £15,000 divided by 20 gives a similar result: £750 per year, just £28 more. £750 or £722, was that what my life experience was worth?

I wasn't happy with either number. Even taking into account the months I had to be carried around, the weeks when I could only crawl, the years when I struggled to learn to speak and tie my shoe laces and get dressed myself. I was making something up and saw no reason why I had to limit myself. What was I worth?

I had already rounded up the numbers I was playing around with, it seemed reasonable to round them up a bit more. What if I was worth £1,000 for each year I'd been alive? That would make the whole thing a lot simpler. £18,000 at age 18. That would mean that I should expect to earn and aim to be earning £20,000 by the time I was 20, £40,000 by the time I was 40. Nice and simple. Easy to remember.

Of course, I was only on £13,000 at the time. This had been a pleasant mental exercise, but I had no plan for how to persuade anyone, let alone my boss, that I deserved a £5,000 increase on my salary.

I can't remember now whether I thought much about how I'd already increased my income by more than £5,000 in under a year. If I did, possibly I also knew that I hadn't done so with a clear plan or knowledge of how that increase was going to come about. I'd been blessed with the job offer. How would I ensure I received another? It would be well over a decade before I was able to answer that question.

Summary

Setting complimentary goals can result in a harmonic effect where working towards each goal can make achieving the other goals easier.

You should be paid a living wage for doing a basic job.

When you go beyond your basic role you should be rewarded for doing so and that any reward should not depend on other team members or departments.

Employees should receive a fairer distribution of profits.

Your skills, knowledge and experience has a value, you should work out what that value is now and what it will be worth in the future.

Prompts and suggestions:

Write down the goals, ambitions and childhood dreams you have had throughout your life.

Which of these do you feel the strongest desire to achieve?

Why do you want to do that?

What inspires you?

Write down your beliefs about wages, salaries, and rewards for the work you do.

Do you feel you are receiving as much as you deserve for the work you do?

Are you willing to work hard, to put in the effort to make yourself more valuable?

The first time I doubled my salary

In the beginning

I was born in Aberdeen on the North East coast of Scotland and my parents moved us all up to the Shetland Isles when I was six. My father was a printer by trade and I learned a lot by working for him as a child on occasional Saturdays and school holidays, also from observing and listening to discussions he had with my mother.

While I enjoyed parts of my experience at school, I can't say those were the happiest years of my life. Having since had experience of higher education, I think that the way we were taught in school was a huge turn off for me. Add to that the fact I was a daydreamer and far more interested in the science fiction stories I read instead of school books, in newly discovered computer games, and most awkwardly in girls and it surprises me I passed as many subjects as I did.

Unable to leave school after fourth year of high school because I hadn't reached the age of 16, I felt I had little choice about going onto fifth year. That meant boarding in Lerwick, the main town on the islands and only 25 miles away, and going to a different school: the Anderson High School.

That was a bad year for me. I was bullied. I struggled with the school work. I got mumps and missed a month of school and the prelim exams. I scraped a pass in Mathematics and Art at Ordinary grade. I ended up getting no award in both English and History at Higher grade, but somehow achieved a Higher grade B pass in Technical Drawing.

As soon as I finished my last exam I was out of school and wanted to never look back.

My Dad arranged an interview with the manager of a local hardware store: The Brae Building Centre. My starting wage: £2.00 an hour.

My annual income after my first year was no more than £4,160.

At the time I knew it wasn't a lot of money, just £80 a week. Out of that I paid my Mum £20 a week towards rent (and bless her, she kept most of it to use to help me out later on when I needed it!)

I learned a lot about plumbing and electrical work simply by talking to the customers and seeing what they bought and finding out why. I had my first taste of driving a forklift (possibly illegally but hey, it was on private land and surely the statute of limitations has passed, right…) I built up my muscles carting gallon tins of paint off trucks to the store room and planks of 2 by 4 to the wood store. Up to this point I'd been a skinny, stunted bookworm and it did me good to do some physical labour.

Hours went by when there was nothing to do. No boss likes seeing their workers standing around doing nothing, so I was given jobs like sweeping the floor, wiping down the shelves and carrying out stock checks. I learned to keep myself busy and gradually found that it was better to just choose to sweep the floor or wipe down the shelves if I had nothing else to do.

Days when there wasn't much trade meant I had time to think. What did I want to do with my life, really? Was I going to be working in this same store in ten years' time? I knew I wanted more than that and couldn't imagine this was going to be a long-term role. I needed to do something else but had no idea what.

Later on, I was given advice to have a five and ten year plan. Even years later I had no idea what that really meant or how to come up with such a thing. All I really knew was that I needed to do more, to be more and I couldn't see it happening where I was.

Actually, that's not entirely true. I did wonder if managing the hardware store could be a possibility. The owner occasionally drove into town to get supplies and once or twice went away on fishing trips. I proved myself worthy of trust and was left in charge of the store more and more during the year and a half that I worked there.

The business was successful. We always seemed to have plenty of trade, even taking into account the slow times. A large part of the business was just making sure we kept the shelves full of whatever the customers were likely to want. On an island, it wasn't like there was a lot of choice for people. If we couldn't supply what they needed, they could go into town themselves, or catch a flight or an overnight boat down to Aberdeen…

But I didn't see pursuing managing the store as being the route I wanted to take. In all honesty I wanted to leave the island, get away and experience more of the world. I may have only been six when I left Aberdeen, but I still felt myself to be a city boy.

So, not having a clue what direction I should take, I started asking questions. I went into the local job centre and careers advice office and asked what possibilities there were.

It turned out I was eligible for a training course—the Youth Training Scheme. I wouldn't be able to complete the full two years due to my age, but it would allow me to get more work experience, get some college certificates and get a completion certificate for the training assuming I passed the minimum modules.

The only issue was I would receive £30 a week, a drop in income of £2,600 or 62%!

Up in the air

When you're not earning much, any drop in income is painful. Despite working a forty-hour week at the Brae Building Centre, I wasn't even earning £100 a week. Sure, back in 1989, £100 a week went a lot further than it does today, but to willingly choose to go from £100 to £30 a week... It wasn't an easy decision, but I had to decide.

At the Brae Building Centre, I had what was effectively a permanent job (though with no written contract) paying what I thought was a guaranteed wage. Although no-one had even hinted at the possibility of career progression, I wondered if I could work towards a situation where my employer might trust me to manage the centre. That would hopefully lead to a higher wage and experience that could prove useful later in life.

The Youth Training Scheme offered no long term guarantees other than a training certificate at the end. I would go from a wage to an allowance: pocket money. The training scheme being offered was unusual. I would be trained as a Technical Librarian. This was something that attracted me to the training. I'd always been a bookworm and held librarians in high regard.

In the end though, there were some more intangible benefits that drew me to the training. I would be working for a helicopter company at an airport. Compared to working in a hardware store, that seemed pretty exciting. I had bombed out of my fifth year at school and was ashamed of my results. A training certificate seemed like a useful way to show that I was capable since university seemed like an impossible dream. I wanted adventure and travel and the training scheme seemed to offer that. Did I mention it was working for a helicopter company...? At an airport...?

I was seventeen, no family to take care of, no mortgage or loans to pay off. If I was going to take a major risk, this seemed like the time to do it.

I signed up and started at British International Helicopters in August 1989.

While the careers office had told me the role I was training towards was Technical Librarian, they weren't really sure what that meant. Based at Sumburgh Airport in the south of the Shetland mainland I was boarding with a family near the airport during the week, paid for by the scheme.

The training scheme turned out to be one of those life changing, best decisions I ever made, kind of deals.

The company took their responsibility seriously and I was placed a few weeks at a time in all their departments and given a chance to work in all areas that I safely and legally could. For some reason I never did get to fly one of their helicopters, though I was again let loose on a forklift truck, after completing the required training...

I started working in their reception doing filing and answering the phone, then had some time in the company's control room, watching and trying to learn as the pilots were guided across the airport and directed to different oil rigs. I spent a couple of weeks at a time working with baggage handlers, shadowing engineers, working in the storeroom, and ultimately looking after the helicopter maintenance manuals.

This is where the title of the course came from: Technical Librarian. I was to be responsible for ensuring the helicopter maintenance manuals were kept up to date. Each helicopter type had several thick binders with extensive and detailed diagrams of electronic circuits, mechanical layout, control mechanisms, frames etc. On a fairly frequent basis these would be updated and we would receive a bundle of new sheets. The old ones had to be removed and the new ones carefully inserted into the correct location.

That part of the job was fairly quickly dealt with and so I annoyed my manager on a regular basis asking him what I could do next. I suspect that is one annoyance most managers would rather they got more of...

Make your manager know you get the job done well and quickly and you are eager for more work. It will either pay off by making a pay rise or promotion more likely or will allow you to build a good relationship that could lead to a valuable reference.

And of course, I got more to do. Some of it boring scut work, but there was something about working at an airport that made all the boring scut work seem like it was the most exciting boring scut work in the whole world. There was a constant buzz around the place and not just from the helicopters.

Engineers were constantly in a flap, trying to make sure the onerous maintenance schedules were adhered to while also dealing with issues that could prevent a helicopter from flying. Helicopters and other aircraft were taking off and landing all day long. Occasionally we got visiting aircraft passing through. A Harrier jump jet and a Hercules transport were two memorable occasions at our relatively small airfield.

Each helicopter had to have a series of maintenance checks and changes made on a rolling schedule. We called these 'P' checks. A P1 check was a fairly minor check ensuring that fluids were topped up, perishable O rings and pins that held equipment in place while on the ground also had to be replaced.

A P2 check was more extensive with all the P1 checks to be carried out and additional checks on systems and components. P3 was more extensive still: components replaced and sent for testing... You get the picture.

P1 checks were carried out daily, P2 weekly, P3 every fifty hours of flying, P4 every 100 hours etc. In many ways it was similar to the maintenance schedule we're supposed to follow for our cars except failure to follow that maintenance schedule could have meant 18 people plunging to their death in the freezing waters of the North Sea.

I began to take an interest in the maintenance schedules. Every morning the chief engineer would look at the week ahead and work out when each check had to be carried out and how many flight hours were remaining until the check was due. Knowing how long the check would take, he would then juggle the schedule to ensure we always had enough aircraft available to fly. As we normally only flew Monday to Friday this meant weekends were busy with maintenance checks. Engineers worked early or late shifts, early shift starting at six in the morning, late shift finishing at ten PM with a cross over during the busiest part of the day. Seven days off, seven days on. Some engineers even did fourteen days off, fourteen days on. I'm not convinced that was a sensible pattern, but hey ho…

I would get my daily chores done and then try and write up the schedule myself each morning, applying what I'd seen the chief engineer and others do in terms of juggling the schedule. Most times the chief would come in, scrub away what I'd written and start again, but even so, I learned a lot about balancing requirements and limitations through that exercise.

Demonstrate your willingness to learn new skills by copying what others do and trying to learn from them.

I also learned that there was a need to ensure parts were in the store in advance of the checks being carried out. If we were short of the required O ring, the most basic check could fail as the part couldn't be replaced.

Having been round each department, I started to find myself without work to do. Knowing that admitting to not having work could lead to keep-him-busy work being doled out, I sought work to do. Engineers were generally too busy to explain what they were doing and other than fetching parts for them I wasn't able to help them.

I had no desire to work in the reception and knew a trainee wasn't going to be allowed to give commands to pilots. I could have spent more time with the baggage handlers, call me a snob if you like but I didn't see any career progression there.

The only other department that showed interest in me was the store. Perhaps because there was only one storeman, and having worked in a hardware store, I felt quite at home there carrying out stock checks, finding equipment that a customer... engineer... wanted, parcelling up parts and ordering parts that we were about to run out of.

I began to spend more and more time in the store and Jack, the storeman, took me under his wing, taught me how the place worked, taught me a healthy disrespect for the engineers, and eventually worked things out so I was offered a job working alongside him.

I imagine every trainee hopes that their training will lead to a job offer. I hadn't imagined that I'd get one within a year of taking the training course, or that the job would pay double what I'd been earning previously.

They placed a lot of trust in me. Aged 18 I was offered a permanent job as a storeman with responsibility for a Bonded store (one where items are tracked and access is restricted) containing helicopter engines, gearboxes, electronic instruments and all manner of parts some of which were valued at an easy £500,000 per part.

We arranged with the training scheme that I could continue to complete the YTS course and still get my certificate. Within one year of leaving my old job I had doubled my income from £4,000 to £8,000. Plus, I got a shift allowance which effectively tripled my income.

A lot of that money was now going on tax, national insurance and a pension contribution but I was still earning significantly more and for the first time in my life began to save money.

Always try to save as much as you can. It doesn't matter how much or how little you are earning, save what you can and you might end up being better off than someone earning more who doesn't save a penny!

Under water

Every employer I've ever worked for on a permanent contract, every financial advisor I've ever talked to, and most supposedly wise authorities on financial matters have told me and will tell you to sign up for a company pension scheme. The benefits are huge. The employer usually pays in an amount, the amount you pay in gets taken off before tax and due to compound interest there are huge benefits to saving in a pension over time.

Unless of course your pension was managed by Robert Maxwell...

When Mr Maxwell jumped (or was pushed) off his yacht back in 1991 I, along with thousands invested in the Mirror Group Pension scheme, lost everything that had been saved in the pension scheme. It made me highly suspicious of pension schemes from that point on and for most of my working life since then I've not had a pension.

The experience I'd had was compounded when my Father shared some years later that his pension had been affected by the Enron scandal that broke in 2001. He'd stopped paying into his pension scheme when he found the value had plummeted.

Legislation around pensions has improved a lot over the last couple of decades, in part because of scandals like Maxwell, and when schemes are run honestly it is still one of the most cost-effective ways to save for your retirement. However, for most of the population, saving for a pension is a luxury. How do you justify locking your earnings away for forty years when you aren't able to save to replace the fridge or washing machine?

At times I've not earned enough to contribute into a pension scheme. When I have, and I've been willing to trust the system, I've always cashed in my money when I've moved to a new job. It's always painful as tax and national insurance is taken off before any money is returned and suddenly you realise just how much of your money goes to the tax man.

I quite like the discipline of saving that pensions help with. Once you've made the decision to save and signed the papers, the money comes out of your salary before tax is paid, reducing your immediate tax bill. That's always a good feeling. Because I've acted like a contractor my whole working life, never staying in one job more than two years, I've been able to cash in any pension I'd saved towards, turning the schemes into medium term savings plans. Those chunks of cash have been very helpful over the years.

However, I'm conscious with every year that goes by that old age is approaching and it's looking less and less likely that the government will be able or willing to support my retirement.

After Maxwell I decided it was unlikely I'd ever be able to retire. You only have to do a bit of reading to understand how the state pension works and realise in the long term its unsustainable. Do you know how it works?

Growing up I was fed the lie that we pay national insurance to save for our pensions in the future. The government perpetuates this myth by telling us that when we don't pay enough national insurance in any one year, we reduce our eligibility towards our future pension.

If that was true, the government would be sitting on an ever-increasing mountain of coin, all the savings that people like you and me have to pay each month through national insurance.

But it's not true. Instead, try researching pension black hole, or pension time bomb…

The truth is that all the national insurance we pay goes towards paying the pensions of those who have already retired. There is no mountain of coin, there is no savings bank for our pensions. We pay it in and the government pays it out.

There's a fair chance that by the time you and I retire, the whole great Ponzi scheme will have dried up and if we haven't put money aside ourselves, we'll just have to keep working until we finally keel over.

This is one of the motivators that has driven me to earn more, to finally feel that I could afford to save for the long term and, in the last couple of years, start paying once again into a pension.

Later on in this book I go on to explain why, in spite of my experiences, I still believe we should all make an effort to save for a pension, and give some illustrations of how it can benefit you.

Old time religion

Settling into my role as storeman at the helicopter company, I had no real ambitions. I briefly considered buying a cottage a colleague was selling for £11,000. I wasn't ready to make that kind of commitment and the location wasn't ideal, but for years afterwards I wondered if I'd let a bargain slip through my fingers. Property can be a great long term investment, however it would have made other decisions harder and given my choices and events a couple of years later, I'm now glad I wasn't tied down.

Several major events occurred during my time at the helicopter company. As part of the YTS, I was sent on an outward-bound course. I was expecting raft building, camping, and hiking. What I found was a classroom-based course designed to teach teenagers how to set up their own business. Before I went, I'd rather have found myself in a forest, but I decided to take as much as I could and ended up enjoying the week and learning some useful ideas. The best thing that came out of that week was a friendship with a girl who a few years later agreed to marry me.

Within a year of that week I also got "religion".

I'd had "religion" for my whole life. Brought up by Christian parents, I knew the Bible inside out and my work ethic was firmly based on principles of hard work, honesty, integrity and respect found in the Bible. I believed then and still do, that anyone who applies the wisdom found in the Bible will reap many rewards in terms of business success.

In 1991 I headed down to England on a working holiday, attending a Christian conference on evangelism, then hitting the streets to tell people about Jesus. While at the conference I experienced what Christians call being filled with the Holy Spirit. While being prayed for I felt warmth and tingling flowing from my head, down through my body, to my hands and feet. I walked out of that place feeling intoxicated and full of joy. I was a Christian before I went on holiday, but by the time I went back to work I had changed and I hadn't realised how much conflict that change would cause.

I was still quite young, only 19 and until then everyone had seemed to get on well enough with me. The only real difference in my behaviour was that I wanted to read the Bible more. So, at lunch, I took my Bible into the crew room and read it. Silently. Like any normal book. I can't remember how long it took, but either on that first day or soon after, one of the engineers threw his newspaper down and walked out. I didn't think anything of it until he walked out the next day, this time when he saw me enter the crew room, and then again on the following day. Up until then he'd been quite happy to talk to me, but just because he saw me reading a Bible, he refused to even be in the same room as me. Most of my colleagues weren't bothered by my decision to read the Bible in public, but for a few, it seemed to be highly offensive.

Possibly because of this, probably also because I found my own conscience was bothering me more, I had more conflict with some engineers. Over a period of weeks I became more assertive which only seemed to cause more issues. One issue in particular brought things to a head.

We frequently had travelling salesmen visit to try and sell cleaning materials. Our helicopters needed a lot of cleaning, the North Sea throwing up corrosive salt water, the aircraft engines staining the fuselage with the exhaust fumes. One of these salesmen brought an incentive, a calendar with photos of some rather attractive young women, topless. My counterpart in the store pinned up the calendar, probably not thinking anything of it. I promptly took it down when I walked in on my first shift of the week.

I didn't think all that much before my actions. Maybe if the calendar had always been there, I wouldn't have noticed, but to be honest, I'd never seen any similar calendars anywhere in the hanger. Growing up I'd enjoyed seeing pictures of naked women while at the same time feeling guilty about it. The two changes in my life meant I didn't want the calendar there. I was perfectly happy with my girlfriend, and my conscience was not going to let me be comfortable looking at the calendar. So I took it down, rolled it up and put it in a locker that only my counterpart and I had the key for.

I thought it wasn't for me to tell my counterpart what he displayed on the walls of the store, but I did not have to look at it while I was there. I didn't think any more about it until one of the engineers asked where the calendar was. Then another, and another, and one or two were quite angry that I'd taken the calendar down.

Most of the engineers were from a military background having served as engineers working on aircraft for the RAF, the Army or Navy. They were all at least a decade older than me, some in their forties and fifties and I had a lot of respect for them. When one of them demanded I put the calendar back up I refused. I was asserting myself only to have a couple of taller, bigger, stronger, older engineers try to shout me down.

Then they demanded I give the calendar to them. Maybe that would have been the wise thing to do at that point, but my conscience wouldn't let me. It wasn't my calendar. I couldn't just hand it over. I also suspected it would be put up somewhere else where I'd have to walk past it. I tried to ride it out, thought things would calm down. Then my Bible went missing.

I'd left it on one of the many desks in the store, but then it wasn't there. At first I wondered if I'd moved it and forgotten, but I hadn't. Finally I realised that because I'd taken their calendar, they had taken my Bible. Now I was really conflicted. Looking back, I wish I'd just sucked it up.

Accepted this as a consequence. I could buy a new Bible. I wasn't going to be bullied.

I gave in, took the calendar to the engineer who'd been most insistent who then told me where the Bible was: in the store! It had only been moved to the back of one of the shelves. I would have found it eventually.

I had some other run-ins with engineers and I don't know who complained or what the complaint even was, but soon after the Base Engineer—my line manager—took me aside for a chat. He'd noticed that I'd changed, said others had noticed I'd changed, and he asked me what had happened.

I can't recall the detail of the conversation. How do you explain what it means to have been filled with the Holy Spirit, to know that God is real, to realise that everything we do has meaning and purpose?

As I wasn't initiating conversations on religious topics, wasn't trying to convert anyone, was simply doing my job, but also publicly choosing to use my free time to read a Bible, there wasn't a lot else to be said.

I wonder what would happen today, what does happen today? I've noticed there are far fewer topless calendars on display in the workplace. Yet it seems to me that there are still some in our workplaces that have a hatred of people who in any way publicly acknowledge they have a faith. I feel there is a need to honour our employers by using the time they pay us for to carry out the work we have to do. Yet if I choose to read the Bible during my lunch break, how does that affect anyone else? If someone else is offended by your faith, I feel that is an issue they need to resolve internally, not one you should be made to suffer for.

Summary

You may need to start in a low paid, entry level job, before you can learn the skills and gain the knowledge you need to progress.

Sometimes an opportunity will present itself for you to gain more skills and experience, but will require you to sacrifice time, money, and/or security. Only you can decide if that opportunity is worth the risk.

Change might be scary, but change is the only way that things can improve.

Save as much as you can and be careful how you invest your savings. It is your money, but there are a lot of people who would like to take it from you.

Prompts and suggestions:

Would you be willing to take a pay cut if it meant getting some valuable training?

Have you explored and asked what career options are open to you?

What are you doing with slack time at your work?

Consider if you have time to do more and if so, ask your manager what you could do to help.

Are you seeking to learn new skills, or better understand what it is your colleagues do?

Have you started saving for your pension or your long term future?

What do you know about the pension scheme?

Apart from reading this book, are you reading any others to improve your knowledge, to help you learn new skills?

Do you agree that hard work, honesty, integrity and respect are principles we should apply at work? Why are these principles important?

What's it all for?

Giving it all up

I wrote in the introduction that Jesus said no-one can serve both God and money. Jesus has had a greater positive influence on the world than anyone before or since. While Jesus warned against putting our trust in money and possessions, he never condemned earning money. Instead, he used the principles of working and saving in many of his parables. Yet he also made it clear that seeking to know God and be obedient to him was more valuable than any salary or wealth.

Still quoted today for his statements like "Judge not less you be judged" and "Love your neighbour as yourself", Jesus last command to everyone who would follow him was that we should go and make disciples as he did. If you want to double your salary, then obeying Jesus final command might seem like the last thing you should do. One of the questions I want to ask in this book however is: what is the most important thing in our lives?

For me in the winter of 1991/92, that was being obedient to Jesus last command. I signed up for a training course with the missionary organization Youth With A Mission early in 1992. I handed in my notice, quit a successful, secure job and headed out to a life of uncertainty and significantly reduced financial prospects. In fact, within a couple of years of tripling my salary I had reduced it to zero!

Was I making a huge mistake?

Well, within two years British International Helicopters lost the lucrative contract to ferry workers out to the North Sea oil rigs and their operation in Sumburgh was all but shut down. I wonder whether my "permanent" job would have been made redundant as a result.

I've had this happen a couple of times in my life where I've left a supposedly secure role for something considerably more risky and uncertain only to find later the secure role became much less so.

Don't assume your current career path is certain to remain on track working for the same company. There are no guarantees in employment.

I left Shetland in the Spring of 1992 with my little Fiat 127 fully fuelled and my suitcase stuffed full. I didn't expect to be returning home any time soon. I completed a five-month training course with Youth With A Mission and then set about asking God what I should go on to do. God was fairly silent.

I heard about a team planning to head out to Uzbekistan, one of the new independent former Soviet Republics, and could have joined them but had no sense God was asking me to do this.

I was invited to return to Shetland and lead a Youth Cafe in a paid position where I would be responsible for raising the funds. In addition to this I had the sense that if God wanted me anywhere, it was home in Shetland. So back I went.

A ten year plan?

Until this point I'd had no real plan for my life. At school I'd nursed a childish dream that I would be a writer, burying this when I realised it wasn't the answer teachers and adults in general were looking for. Once you leave school, it seems that people have less interest in asking the question: what do you want to do with your life? If you'd asked me how I felt about that, I suspect back then I'd have been quite relieved.

I had no plan. I'd left school disillusioned with education, I'd signed up for a training course with no long term guarantees and you could argue that I'd stumbled into a well-paid job. I'd then left this job to follow an internal conviction that life was about more than money. In September 1992 I still had that conviction, but wasn't sure what "life was about more" meant.

I know people who seem to have a very clear sense of God speaking to them and I've always been envious of them. For me, I believe God answers my requests when he feels it is right to do so, and other than giving me general guidance expects me just to get on with things. Most of the time I'm quite happy with this arrangement, but there are times when I've just wanted to be told what to do.

But why should I want this? Sure, it might be easier if our creator gave us a list of instructions, but since humanity has shown itself quite incapable of doing what we're told, I suspect God wants us to develop the maturity to decide things for ourselves.

In my short term future I'd made one commitment, to become the youth leader of The Alternative Cafe. The only downside was that I was responsible for raising the funds that were going to pay the £50 a week I would earn as a youth leader. Just over £200 a month, a far cry from the £1,000 a month I'd been earning at the helicopter company!

I set about trying to raise funds and as you might expect, asked the youth and young adults who used the cafe for their suggestions. I can't recall who suggested kidnapping a minister from one of the local churches, but that idea grew until it couldn't be stopped.

We ended up asking several ministers if they would agree to be sponsored to being kidnapped, with the individual receiving the most sponsorship being the victim.

Surprisingly, I don't recall any refusals and soon we had four ministers listed and the youth out hunting for sponsors.

While planning a kidnapping was a lot of fun, I felt that I should let the police know what we were doing in case we were interrupted in the act. I'm not sure what the desk officer thought when I rolled up informing him I was planning a kidnap, but they took it in their stride, took my details and I didn't end up in a jail cell.

We ended up linking the kidnapping to a "lock in", an event some youth groups use where you stock up on snacks, plan games, rent some movies and plan to stay up all night.

And the plan grew.

By the week before we'd planned our abduction, the Baptist minister had won the sponsorship by a clear majority. A couple of members of our team suggested they should pretend to be a couple in need of counselling and they would go to the minister's house before the agreed time to keep him occupied and prevent him from running away. A few days after I called the minister to let him know his congregation had been extremely generous and confirm the date, our fictional couple made an appointment for early that same evening.

They duly turned up and spun a story, then we turned up earlier than we'd advised, water pistols in hand, rope and a blindfold ready, bursting into the room where the counselling session was taking place. I look back and wonder how we got away with it. The minister was, quite understandably, furious at us bursting in on the counselling session. Then the "couple" pulled out water pistols of their own...

We placed the blindfold over his head, tied his hands behind him and led him out. Across the street I saw people exiting another church. I hope that a call was made, though never found out. Perhaps that advance warning I'd given the police averted a response. I can't imagine that we would ever now be allowed to get away with it all.

It seemed a long walk to the centre where we planned to have the lock in, gingerly leading the minister down the cobbled street.

I confess that I left him tied up once we got there, longer than I should have. I hadn't scripted any further than the kidnapping and was now out of my depth. Fortunately, the other ministers and wives had their own plan. They started banging on the doors of the centre demanding the release of our hostage. Negotiations were brief, I was glad to release the hostage and not have to worry about him. We settled in for the night, though I seem to recall that by the early hours, most of us had given up on the idea of staying up all night.

We organised a few more fund-raising events, and though none came close to the kidnapping, income from the fund raising and donations from churches allowed me to earn my way through the year.

But £50 a week doesn't go far, even when you are back living with your parents.

Did I mention my Dad was a printer? Having had a disastrous last year of school I'd developed a distrust of and animosity towards education. I'd decided that common sense and hard work and life experience were far more useful. Working hard is not something I learned at school, I learned it at my father's side, working with him digging the garden, and cutting and bringing home peat to fuel our fire and stove, working for him in his printing business as a child. I learned from him how to keep going when my fingers and arms were tired. How to turn boring and repetitive tasks into games that staved off the boredom. How to use competition between workers to increase productivity. Above all, I learned to enjoy working and then being rewarded for hard work with money and respect.

That year back in Shetland I worked again for my father. He'd had hopes that I might work permanently alongside him, but our relationship had been too volatile as I was growing up for me to trust that I could work long term for him. Instead, after a few years working for other employers, I'd learned to respect his skill and the way he and my mother managed the business, battling against the usual issues that small business owners face.

In addition to the five hours a week I'd work at the Youth Cafe, I'd also agreed I'd work part time for my local church and be paid a small amount. The three jobs together took up all my time and paid enough that I could start saving. I was earning again, less than at the helicopter company, but more than I had been at the hardware store.

I've experienced that same situation more than once, earning more, then less, then more again. I'm sure if money was my only motivator then I could see a more consistent trend upwards in my income, but I've never wanted money to be the sole reason I worked. I've always looked for opportunity, for adventure, and for purpose.

As part of working for the church I was given the opportunity to receive mentoring from Rev Ian Thomson, another Baptist minister.

Several times over that year Ian asked me what my long-term plans were. I had no real idea. The future was a grey mist. He recommended I consider writing or creating both a five-year plan and ten-year plan.

At the age of twenty I didn't know where to begin. It was only after I reached the age of thirty that I began to realise how important Ian's advice was. Back in the winter of 1992/93 however, my thoughts were elsewhere…

Hitched

I stayed in Shetland for less than a year. I'd met my future wife, Teri, a few years previously when she lived at the opposite end of Scotland from me, separated when I lived in Shetland by a twelve-hour boat trip and four-hour drive. Then, after we'd been in a long-distance relationship for six months, she moved 500 miles further south to London to study. I didn't take any hint...

We eventually set a date for our wedding after the summer, in 1993. Teri was doing what was called a "sandwich course" degree where she worked for six months every summer during the first three years of her course. If you're still in school considering university, then a sandwich course can give you anywhere up to a year and half of paid work experience, in some cases more valuable than the degree!

In the spring, I decided I would leave Shetland to look for work near where Teri was working allowing me to spend more time with her in the lead up to the wedding and prepare for living together. When you don't know any better you can make some dumb decisions.

Teri was in Yorkshire. We were going to get married in Argyll, then return to Yorkshire for a few weeks, then head to Uxbridge where she would continue her studies.

I had no idea how difficult it would be to get any kind of job when I was planning to move every few weeks for the near future. I did the usual, signing up at the local Job Centres, applying for work that I had experience of, but the fact was that I had very little experience and no-one was hiring for the jobs I could do. If I'd known or maybe had advice, I possibly could have found work as a day labourer, but I didn't know where to start looking, or even that I should be looking.

As a result, I hardly worked that summer and probably should have just stayed in Shetland. Though having been happily married now for twenty-five years, I'm going to say those extra weeks I spent with my future wife were worth the loss in earnings.

We married in 1993 while she was half way through her university degree. Moving from Shetland to London, I took the first job I could get in the town of Uxbridge and we scraped by for the next two years.

That job in Uxbridge was the first role where I was responsible for other people. Twenty-one years old and I had managed to become a supervisor in a small hospital laundry catering primarily to Care of The Elderly wards. Only a small team of two people and only on part time (22.5) hours, but it seemed like a career progressing move working for the NHS. Except I was woefully unprepared to manage other people. Within a couple of weeks I managed to offend both members of my team as I tried to assert my new-found authority.

I wasn't trying to pick a fight, but I ended up starting one and it gave me a harsh lesson in unintended consequences. Since then I've learned a lot about how people handle change including change in authority. I may have avoided that situation but there could have been a different trigger later on.

That event shattered my confidence. Though I later had the opportunity to lead other teams, it took me a decade to believe I was capable of managing other people again.

While it took me years to realise it, I did learn at the time, did adapt and looking back, I think I ended up a pretty good supervisor. I learned to listen to my team. I learned to seek their advice and then promote their ideas. I worked hard to understand the job realising that my role wasn't to be in charge, but to work alongside them, and to support them.

It was in that role that I first carried out what I now know is a business analysis. A constant complaint from the team was that we had too much work to do. Initially I wondered if that was just standard griping found in many organisations. Eventually though as I observed the work being done and questioned my team about how their work had changed, I realised that they were right.

Fortunately, the previous supervisor had kept good records and we had kept on recording what we were doing. With some analysis I was able to show that while our hours had remained constant, our workload had increased by some thirty percent.

Tying this fact together with analysis that showed we were consistently under budget I put together a proposal to use that budget surplus to increase our hours. The proposal was accepted and we were able to redistribute our hours to better manage the workload. And all this without a computer to crunch the numbers…

Don't panic

As the two-year anniversary of starting the supervisor role approached, my wife was completing her degree. Although our relationships within the team had improved tremendously, I still found the job stressful and I was worried about the immediate future. My wife and I had spent her last year living in university married flats accommodation which had cost us far less than renting, but quite soon we were going to have to leave and our costs would rise.

My wife was applying for jobs based all around the country and we knew we might have to move but not where to. My part time job wasn't enough to support both of us and we had very little savings. Stress, uncertainty and worry finally caught up with me one morning as I sat at my small desk in that hospital laundry. I became very aware of my breathing and started to feel like there was pressure on my chest. One of my team took me up to A&E where I sat feeling foolish for an hour before someone could see me.

I was having a panic attack. Nothing major, life had simply got too much for me.

I'm stubborn. To the point where I will stick things out way past the point a normal person would quit. That panic attack shook me and made me finally admit that the stress I was under in the job was unhealthy for me.

I still believe that it is right to tough things out, to give difficult situations a chance to improve, yet there also needs to be wisdom deciding when enough should be enough.

If a child of mine ever does what I did next, I hope I can trust it is the right thing for them. I quit my job.

I had no job to go to. My wife had no job offers. We did have one thing going for us though. We worshiped a God who had promised to provide for us.

There is a passage in the book of Matthew that followers of Jesus sometimes glibly quote. In this passage

Jesus tells us not to worry. Not about our lives, not what we will eat or drink and not about what we will wear. Why? Because we have a father in heaven who knows we need these things. Jesus goes on to tell us to seek first God's kingdom and God's righteousness and the things we need will be given to us as well as God's kingdom and God's righteousness. Then Jesus rounds it all off by saying don't worry about tomorrow for tomorrow will worry about itself! How does that make you feel?

At times it scares the living daylights out of me, but back in late 1995 I had to live by that passage. And though my wife must have wondered what she had signed up for when I told her I thought I had to quit my job and though many people must have thought me foolish, it turned out that we never wanted for our lives or for food or drink or clothes or any of the many other things that we needed.

The church we had been going to—Hillingdon Park Baptist Church—had been left a house in a will, and they allowed us to stay in it rent free once we had to leave the university accommodation.

My wife attended several interviews the week before I was due to officially leave my job and on my last day of work she called me to say she'd had a job offer!

I don't believe for a minute that God waves his hand and conjures up whatever we want in any circumstance. My wife studied hard to get her degree. She was able to get work experience during her degree and proved herself a capable employee. I do believe that God works with what we give him. If we give him excellence, then he uses excellence. If we give him rubbish then while he can still turn that rubbish into something good, it will not be the same as if we had given all we could have.

I got home full of relief only to have my wife tell me she didn't want to take the job!

You can maybe imagine that my stress levels took a hit that evening.

What? What!?

The job offer was based in Grimsby and while she'd worked there before, and we'd lived there for a few weeks after we were first married, she wanted to hold out to hear if she would get a different offer for a role with more potential based in York.

She wasn't due to hear until Monday, so we spent a long weekend hoping the York offer would come through and hoping that if it didn't the Grimsby offer would still be on the table.

Visions and Dreams

I've wanted to write stories since I was eight. Do you know what is wrong with that statement?

Quite simply it should have been: I've been writing stories since I was eight!

I've always been a daydreamer. I wasted much of my school years in what in Shetland is colloquially known as a "dwam". Dreams are good, but if you spend all your time dreaming about the future and never work towards getting there, you'll find you are stuck where you are.

My wife was offered the job in York. She accepted and we moved there late 1995. I had a succession of part time jobs—my full CV doesn't even mention them all as some of them only lasted a couple of days. While I wasn't working I tried to make some breakthrough on my childhood dream of being a writer. I struggled to earn £9,000 a year.

Despite my antagonism towards education, I'd continued studying after I left school, ashamed of how poorly I'd done. I scraped a C pass in Physics at night school. I later got a B pass in Biology while considering applying for a career in Nursing. (I've often taken training or returned to education to try and aid my career, frequently to then find it wasn't the right direction to take.) I was rejected in my application to go to London Bible College when I still was considering becoming a missionary. They advised I took some correspondence courses to verify if I was up to higher level study. I did quite well at that and gained an average grade of 90% in the one correspondence course I tried, far higher than I'd achieved at school.

Through it all I had no real direction, no ambition other than an undefined dream that I wanted to write stories and make a living from it.

Then a couple of things happened that changed our lives for ever. The first of these was being asked by friends to consider joining them on a team heading out to Central Asia. They were planning to work with a charity, a Non-Governmental Organization (NGO) called the Central Asian Development Agency that was operating in Tajikistan, the smallest of the Central Asian former Soviet republics. When the Soviet Union collapsed, several former republics declared independence. Some went on to prosper, but Tajikistan did not. Civil war broke out shortly after independence and much important and vital infrastructure was disrupted: roads, telephone lines, even water supplies were affected.

Civil war brought poverty and for a land-locked country dominated by two mountain ranges, trading was difficult and usable land scarce. There was a clear need for basics like food and clothes, also for practical help towards repairing infrastructure and establishing businesses in a country where the State had previously been responsible for everything.

A decade before I'd considered working in neighbouring Uzbekistan. Now I was being offered an opportunity to provide practical help to people who needed it. The Bible is full of teaching advising us to be kind to the poor and those in need. The adventure appealed to me, also I still had a sense of calling to go, yet I resisted this new invitation to travel to Central Asia. When it came down to it, I wasn't ready to just go.

After some months we agreed to join them on a month long "look and see" visit along with ten others who were considering the invitation. We distributed clothes and shoes and heavy bags of flour. We shopped in the local bazaars, got violently sick when we didn't follow all of the health advice we'd been given—or maybe in spite of it. We learned a few words in the local language, visited towns and villages and got an insight into what life might be like if we joined the team.

Then we went home and struggled to decide what to do. We asked God. God seemed to be silent. Then the second life changing event occurred. My wife became pregnant.

Children have a way of bringing reality home. I knew that I wanted to be sure I could provide for my kids. Years later, as they got older, I realised that I wanted to be able to help them if they wanted to go to college or get married in the future, just the same as our parents had. And of course, if we decided to join the team, it would be very different doing so with a child.

It would have been easy to use having a child as an excuse to make the decision for us. We knew Tajikistan was a dangerous place. We knew we had got sick when we were there before. We knew we would be giving up the NHS, 24-hour supermarkets, our home and friends and family.

Yet Jesus addressed many concerns like these, challenging all who would claim to follow him that giving up homes and families was part of the deal. And the thought of making an excuse over such an important decision didn't sit right with me. I would have to live with the decision for the rest of my life and I wanted to make the right one. But in the absence of a voice from heaven or an angelic command, how did I decide what to do?

I just didn't know how to decide. Months went by and then my friends challenged me with an illustration that our lives are like ships on the ocean with God at the helm. We might want God to steer our lives, but how can he do that when we are not moving? It's only once the ship begins to move that it can be steered.

I suspect that God wanted me to make the decision. He is quite happy to give us directions, but doesn't want us to be like puppets. He might not like the decisions we make, but even a decision he knows is not best for us, sets us on a course that he can offer direction from.

I decided that we would commit to going and if God was going to bless us, he would. If we were heading in the wrong direction, he would warn us. I was finally moving!

Tajikistan

I'd fund raised before, writing letters, meeting with church ministers, organising fund-raising events, asking people to consider supporting me. Twice. First when I left my work to join Youth With A Mission and then when I returned to Shetland to become a youth leader.

We worked out that we needed roughly £12,000 a year to cover flights, accommodation, food and all the other expenses we would have. We asked our family and friends if they would consider supporting us. We broke down the sum we thought we needed and let everyone know that if 100 people pledged to give £10 a month, we could afford to go. Or, if 50 people gave £20 a month, or if 25 people gave £40 a month…

It's something you now see charities doing almost every day. Text this number now to give £3 and save a child's life. If you give £5 a month this village can have clean water. You break the big number down into something people can understand and afford and if they believe in what you are doing, they will support you.

If they believe in what you are doing…

I wasn't sure what would happen. Either people would consider supporting us or they would not. Either way I would see as confirmation that either God would bless our decision or he would not. We visited half a dozen churches, contacted everyone we knew and within a few months had enough pledges that we could afford to go. We signed up with the Central Asian Development Agency (CADA) and agreed I would work with them. We got our visas. We left and arrived in Tajikistan before our team was ready for us!

The next two years were an adventure. We experienced hospitality, kindness, friendship from the Tajik people. There were a few times we were in fear for our lives. Our team experienced problems and tragedies, along with many blessings. Our second child was born just over a year after we went out. We returned to the UK for the birth, then returned after a short furlough.

Living long term in Tajikistan with children was very different from a month-long experience without them. It was a lot harder for my wife who was stuck at home while I worked in the office or went travelling, something I tried not to do too often as it was still dangerous to travel through some areas, law and order not having fully returned after the civil war.

After Tajikistan declared independence from the Soviet Union in 1991, the country split along ethnic and regional lines, the Eastern half of the country finding itself the losers in the formation of a new government. Groups from the area around the city of Garm and the region of Gorno-Badakhshan tried to also declare independence from Tajikistan. Even in 1999, two years after the civil war officially ended, and into 2000 there were still flare ups with attacks and fighting.

Our first year in country we carried radios wherever we went, alert to advice to avoid certain places and to maintain curfews. My role at CADA was managing five email centres located in Tajikistan's major cities, though the local managers did most of the managing perfectly well. It might seem hard to believe now that an email centre can have been a thing, but even in the UK in 1999, few people had their own email address, let alone access to the Internet.

In Tajikistan where the civil war had damaged phone and power lines throughout the country, families and businesses were using our email centres to keep in touch and ensure they could communicate with customers and suppliers.

CADA funded the charitable side of providing email to Tajik citizens for free by charging other NGOs, government agencies and local businesses to use our service which to them also included Internet access. This provided an invaluable service to these organizations enabling them to communicate with the outside world. The costs to us of providing this service were considerable and we had to manage the project almost as a business to ensure it could remain viable. In order to connect to the World Wide Web we obtained a satellite feed which took up a large proportion of our budget. We were still reliant on the local telephone lines to connect each city. Fortunately email could be sent from a user's computer to a local server in our email centre, then stored there until the telephone lines were working. As the infrastructure improved we were able to increase the times we connected to send and receive emails and eventually able to allow dial up Internet access to those who could afford to pay for it. Our telephone bills were high as was our electricity bills. If there was ever surplus from our income to the project this was then used to support additional aid projects.

Our trip back to the UK in 2000 was useful to see how much the use of Internet had changed even in a year. Despite all the worry about the Millennium Bug, I was able to see that many more people were using the Internet and that as connection speeds were increasing (most people still had dial up modems) prices were falling.

On my return to Tajikistan I began to realise that the model we had been using to charge customers for their use of email and Internet was unsustainable. We had been charging paying customers for data used. This was a fine model when access to the Internet was restricted, data usage was low and there was no competition. Even in the UK, at the time of writing, this model is still used by mobile phone providers. However, usage of the Internet was changing faster than we could have predicted. Our model didn't allow for the possibility that users might not restrict their data usage and so the cost to some customers ramped up considerably to the point where they could not afford to pay their bills. We had to adapt our pricing to meet the changing situation, sometimes writing off bills that we would never be paid.

In addition, there were rumours of local companies setting up their own Internet service. Perhaps sooner than we realised, we would start to face competition and then we would be faced with the possibility that we might be holding back the development of local Internet provision unless we scaled down our operations.

On a training course while we were out of the country, I'd been shown how to model a business plan using a spreadsheet. I spent several weeks gathering information on how much we were charging for our services, how much it cost us to provide those services, where we were experiencing difficulties collecting payment, and what competition we faced.

I ended up with a huge spreadsheet with many rows and columns that painted a bleak picture of the project's future. I could see that we would have to reduce our income projections and ultimately scale back the project. I didn't want to share the spreadsheet as it felt like an acknowledgement of failure. I've always wanted to offer suggestions and proposals to make something work rather than give up on it. Yet when I did give the spreadsheet to CADA's Director, he thanked me. His actual words were: "This is something I can use."

I didn't realise it at the time, but I'd just carried out a business analysis and there were a lot of positives that could be taken from the negative projections.

- We were a charitable organization and needed to act in a way that benefitted the whole community. This included not undercutting local competitors and holding customers back from them.

- Our own Email and Internet project needed to be managed well, even if that management meant planning to reduce our services and make local staff redundant.
- Other projects that were benefitting from any funding surplus needed to be able to plan for a time that surplus would not be available.
- Other options could be considered such as spinning off the project into a locally owned stand alone business.

The analysis allowed the Director to develop a more realistic plan for the project's future.

One night I had been driving home, later than planned having stopped to buy pizza at the newly opened, first take-away pizza place in Dushanbe. I slowed down as I saw men standing on the road outside my house. Drew to a halt as they pointed guns at me. Long rifles and automatic machine guns.

I wound down my window as a man in a balaclava shone a torch in my face. I never learned Russian and so didn't understand what he asked me. Instead I'd learned Tajik, the local language. It wasn't the first time I'd been stopped. Usually it was the local police who always softened when they realised I spoke Tajik and not Russian. I did as I always did and answered in Tajik. Told him I was going home then pointed. That was my home, right there. I was allowed to drive on and could feel their eyes on me as I got out of the van I was in, opened the gates to our house and drove inside.

More than half a dozen heavily armed men stopping cars outside our house. That was scary enough. I bolted and padlocked the gate, thankful for the wall that circled our property. Hustled inside having forgotten the pizza. I made sure the doors were locked and then got on the radio. Then we heard someone moving about outside.

The wall wasn't high, it would have been no problem for one of the men to look over, see no-one around and hop over to check things out. We kept on the radio and eventually someone got the local police to drive out. By the time they did, the men had gone.

Partly because of that experience and partly because a section of our wall collapsed in an earthquake soon after, I had a taller wall built. However I made the rookie mistake of not getting proper legal advice and help. Thinking my language skills had improved sufficiently I tried to obtain permission to extend our property, buy some extra land and build a new wall around it which we could use as a garden.

I thought everything had gone well. I received a document, in Russian so I couldn't even begin to translate it, which I believed stated we owned the land. The wall was built and I started to feel a little safer. Then the local police turned up. Three of them. Two with AK-47s. They wanted me to come with them. I didn't know if I was being arrested, but the guns kind of gave that impression. I told Teri, in English, to take the kids to a friends house as soon as we'd left and told her to pray.

It was a surreal experience. The police first drove to a block of flats where a bag of flour was loaded into the boot of the car. Then I was driven to a police station and taken into a fairly large office with a dozen or more men seated round the room. The lights were off and the curtains drawn and I remember the room being shadowed and gloomy. I was told to sit next to the chief, a large man who I think then tried to threaten me.

It's probably a lot easier to threaten someone if they speak your language well, though I was already pretty scared. I did pick up that my wife wouldn't see me for a long time, that she would be crying. I understood that the document I'd paid for didn't seem to be recognised in the same way I'd hoped and that I'd probably broken a law or two.

There had been quite a few times I'd probably broken a law or two in Tajikistan. For a country recovering from civil war, it had seemed like a lawless place when we arrived in 1999. Then gradually the law began to take back control. I'd legally obtained a permit to drive when I arrived, but didn't fully understand the differences between UK and Tajik driving law. I kept being pulled over. There was a suspicion that sometimes this was just to obtain a bribe, and so I'd developed a stock response. I apologized, asked forgiveness, asked for a ticket and declared my willingness to pay. This either stumped and pleased them because the foreigner who looked Russian was choosing to use their language, or called their bluff as they hadn't actually a valid reason to stop me, or resulted in a ticket book being taken out and I settled my account.

I used my stock response, threw in every term I could think of to show my regret and my willingness to resolve the matter. However I wasn't, even under threat of prison, going to pay a bribe. I didn't state this explicitly, but as I kept asking for a ticket (the only word I knew to describe an official penalty) it must have become clear that either I was stupid, or stubborn. Maybe a little of both.

Eventually I was driven back and I then sought out CADA's help to fix the problem I'd caused. Events like these were easy enough to laugh off after a day or two with the adrenaline always kicking in, but the stress did build up. In the spring of 2001 I started to feel pain in my belly. Somehow the umbilical stump under my belly button had become infected. I ended up having an operation locally to investigate, then being medevaced back to the UK to have the stump, and my belly button removed. We took the precautions we could, but sometimes it just wasn't enough.

In August 2001, the leader of the Tajik opposition to the Taliban was assassinated in Northern Afghanistan, an event that was noteworthy, but at the time we didn't understand why. It was only later, after the world changing event of 9/11 had also altered our lives, that the assassination was seen as a tactical measure in the Taliban's efforts to conquer Afghanistan.

A Tajik friend called us during, what was for us, the evening of 9/11 and told us to turn on the TV. He said a plane had flown into a building. Within a few days there was talk of the Americans declaring war on the Taliban in Afghanistan. Russian military presence in Tajikistan started to increase in response. We were concerned that the Russians would see an American attack on Afghanistan as a threat and respond. No-one knew what would happen next. We made preparations to leave. I could not envisage taking the risk of staying if war did break out on neighbouring Afghanistan.

We left early October 2001.

The next months were hard. We were homeless and without purpose. Traumatic experiences from the previous year kept us awake at night. Our children were unsettled, even more because we had to keep moving from place to place.

Eventually we were able to settle back into our old home in York. For over a year we held onto the hope that we could go back to Tajikistan, but it wasn't to be. We continued to receive financial support and I took a part time job on minimum wage manning the UK office of a travel company that a member of our team set up: The Great Game Travel Company. It was good to keep a connection to the country we had planned to give many years to, but I struggled knowing that I wasn't able to fully provide for my family without the support of others. For a couple of years, I felt I was an utter failure.

Summary

Money is important, but should not rule your life.

There are no "secure" jobs. Investing in your own skills and knowledge is vital as you develop your career.

Unless you are applying for a senior role or one that is highly skilled, it is unlikely you will be considered unless you live locally.

You will make mistakes, have conflict with colleagues, feel like a failure. Acknowledging and learning from mistakes, working through conflict, and overcoming failure will all enable you to mature as a person, and be better able to take on more challenging roles.

Not all stress is good.

Dreaming about your future without working towards it will get you nowhere.

Following your "destiny" may result in suffering.

Prompts and suggestions:

If you were made redundant, how would this affect you?

If you had to start over, what might you choose to do instead?

Get two pieces of paper. On one write down: "My five-year plan", on the other write: "My ten-year plan". Now try and imagine what you want to be doing in five- and ten-years' time.

Have you ever wanted to manage other people?

Do you allow your job and life outside work to cause you stress?

How do you deal with stress?

How do you decide what to do in difficult situations?

Have you ever worked out, in detail, the minimum you need to live on?

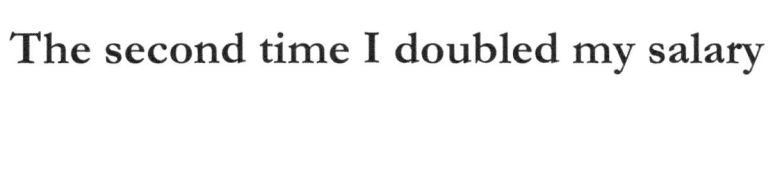

The second time I doubled my salary

When you're at the bottom there's only one direction to take

Early in 2003 we returned to Tajikistan for a three-week trial. Every step was a struggle. We travelled to Kazakhstan, expecting to get a visa for Tajikistan allowing us to travel onwards, but the visa was held up. We all caught colds and spent a miserable week in limbo. When we finally made it to Tajikistan we had no sense that we belonged there. Eventually we decided we would not return and said our goodbyes.

I think we needed those weeks. For two years we had lived with uncertainty over our future. I felt we were barely surviving, emotionally and financially, still accepting charity from family and friends just so we could get by. We had no long-term direction, no plan. I thought a lot about what had happened and wondered how others I had known in Tajikistan had seemed to manage so well.

They seemed to have knowledge I didn't have. They knew how to organise and plan. While I struggled, they seemed to prosper. They had visions for their roles and I couldn't see how I could develop my own vision or systems or methods. I didn't even have the words at that point to know how to describe what I didn't have.

For all my adult life up to that point I had looked down on further education. I freely admit now that this was a response to doing so poorly at school, to being turned down by the institutions I'd applied to. I'd created a fake persona that sometimes talked about my having studied at the University of Life and having done well.

Well… Mostly well.

Perhaps okay.

Actually, I finally had to admit that I was struggling.

On returning, we were able to start to think about the future. My wife began applying for jobs and was accepted for one.

I started to wonder if I should consider trying to get a degree. Began looking at courses and options, finding out how much it would cost. At the same time, I wondered instead if I should get some sort of apprenticeship. Perhaps train in a practical skill. There was apparently a nationwide shortage of plumbers. I had done some DIY plumbing and was confident that with proper training I could be a plumber.

But was that what I really wanted to do? Did I really want to be crawling under floorboards and working with icy water in the winter aged fifty? Or at sixty-five?

No, not really.

I remembered that back in 1996, a former colleague had been studying towards a Higher National Certificate (HNC) in Computing at night school. Looking back I regretted not seizing the initiative and signing up myself back then. But I couldn't have known and maybe would not have benefitted at that time as much as I eventually did.

I'd always been interested in computers and technology and at school had even taken a computing course. Ironically, I'd dropped out of the course when I was too proud, or ashamed to admit, I didn't know how to complete a graded assignment to develop a database. I knew I needed direction in my life, began to believe that if I didn't invest time in training that I would always struggle, and I knew deep down that I was capable of more. I just didn't know what that was or how to get there.

I eventually opted to study towards an HNC in Computing. It seemed to be the most cost-effective way to get a higher education certificate. Certainly it was the quickest as I could have signed up to do the course in one year; but I wanted to see if I could use my experience of being in Tajikistan to write a travel guide to the country and so opted to do the course over two years as a night class. I threw myself into researching while studying in the evenings and weekends. In addition to the support we continued to receive from friends and family, we had signed up for a new government benefit—Tax Credits—while I'd been working for the travel company. The extra money we received kept us going, though I was constantly uneasy at how dependent we were on what I considered to be charity.

I wasn't too uneasy to apply for and—because our income was so low—receive a grant to cover the first year's tuition!

Within a few weeks of starting the course, I knew I'd done the right thing. I fell in love with Systems Analysis and Design: the means by which real life and business processes are mapped out to design a computer system. I took to database design like a duck to water. Whether I'd changed since my experience at school twenty years earlier, or databases had become easier to work with or a lot of both I don't know, but I began to wonder if having a long-term aim to be a systems analyst was a good idea.

We were taught theory and given plenty of practical experience of programming, database design, and networking. We were also introduced to esoteric subjects like Human Computer Interface design: a fancy way of describing the theory of making computers easy to use.

It wasn't all plain sailing. While I had some great tutors who knew their subjects and more importantly, were able to convey their passion and experience in a way that I enjoyed learning from them, there were some sessions where I felt I'd been transported back to High School and I had to fight to make myself interested in topics that seemed duller than dust.

The biggest problem I had during the two years was when one tutor didn't mark our assignments. We had to complete two assignments in order to pass each module, a smaller one and a more complex one. My understanding was that if we did poorly in the smaller assignment, we could identify our weakness in that subject and aim to improve it for the more complex assignment.

I handed in my first assignment on time and expected to get a grade back in a couple of weeks. Those weeks went by, and then another, and another. By this time, I'd already started working on the second assignment which took the work we'd done for the first and built on it. My dilemma was that I wasn't certain that the approach I'd taken for the first assignment was correct.

The way the grading was done, we could scrape a pass on the first assignment and still go on to get at least a merit grade from the second. But if I failed the first, I was worried I would make similar mistakes that would cause me to fail the second. After several weeks of asking the tutor if the assignments had been marked, I gave an ultimatum. I told them it was unacceptable to fail to mark our assignments and that I would need the mark back by the next week.

I suspect that many younger students would not have known how to deal with the situation. I wasn't even sure. I simply knew I had a responsibility to do something. It was incredibly awkward, to know this person was responsible for marking my work, that if I became their enemy, that my grade could suffer. Yet, they had a responsibility and were not doing their job.

By the following week, the assignment had been graded and despite my fears, I went on to gain a distinction in that module.

Talking with other students it has become clear that people with life experience, who know why a further education course will benefit them, are far more likely to do well at college and university than a school leaver. There is a quantum jump in the rationale behind education between school and college/university. It is the difference between learning because you are forced to and learning because you want to. At school we were told what to do, we had no choice in the subjects we studied (certainly up to our second year of high school). We were instructed and guided every step of the way. From the moment you walk into a college or university, you are expected to manage your own learning. Yes, good institutions do help with the transition, but it is a mistake to think anything other than "I am responsible for my own learning."

It is the difference between heading straight home after class and heading to the library to find relevant books on the subjects you are studying. It is the difference between simply writing the assignment then handing it in and setting out to understand exactly what is expected of you then honing and editing your submission to go beyond what has been asked. The difference between thinking the lecturers are there to teach you and realising you are there to learn.

The HNC I studied at York College had a really clear grading system that gave clear expectations and targets. For the first time in my life, I enjoyed the learning process, I soaked it all up, and thanks in large part to that clearly documented grading system, managed to gain distinctions in nine out of ten modules.

While my first year of college was a success, I was struggling with my plan to write a travel guide. I knew I really needed to go back out to Tajikistan and would have needed to spend one or more months travelling the country, but the cost was too high, both in terms of money and, more importantly, being away from my family. Stress and trauma from our time in Tajikistan had taken their toll. I did some research and eventually found that even if the book was eventually published it was highly unlikely to even pay back the costs of fully researching it. Since we did not have the funds to pay for travel and additional research, in the end I chose to abandon the project.

The chocolate coding factory

Half way through the two-year HNC course I got a call from one of my tutors. A local company needed an Excel programmer for a two-week contract. Was I interested? Yes, I was.

The pay was an astonishing £12 per hour. Higher than I'd ever earned in my life. More than my wife had even been earning with her first job after University! If you multiply that hourly rate by 40 hours a week and were able to work 46 weeks a year you could earn £22,080. Okay, so this contract was only for two weeks, but was this really how much Excel programmers got paid?

My client for that first IT contract was Nestle Rowntree. The two-week contract was extended when they asked me to do additional work and I ended up working for them for six months, spending time in several of the manufacturing units for Aero, Polo, Drifter, Smarties and others. I got to see how these sweets are put together and was given a fair few samples to take home. I thought I'd arrived. Then, as quickly as it had started, the funding ran out and I was given notice. However, I now had some genuine IT experience to put on my CV and I'd almost finished the HNC.

I wasn't able to find any other work for a few weeks and I then applied for a temp job that seemed related: redesigning a rota system in Excel for the Crown Prosecution Service. The only issue was they were paying a third less than the last contract: £8 an hour.

They offered me the job and I took it, knowing we needed the money. Again, the job was only for two or three weeks and I busily started applying all I'd learned about systems analysis. I asked dozens of questions, took copious notes during that first week and gradually began to panic!

I had started the week before Easter. I wasn't working the Friday or Monday of Easter Weekend and on the Thursday evening confessed to my wife that there was no way I could possibly do everything they wanted in just three weeks. My wife is usually the sensible one when life throws a curve-ball and she reasonably said that I would just have to tell them it would take longer.

That was fine, but I was worried they would end my contract and find someone else who could complete the project in a shorter time. I didn't have enough experience then to know how long a project would take. I certainly didn't think I had the experience to produce a realistic estimate. But I had gained some skills and knowledge that would turn out useful.

A tutor on the HNC course had—tongue partly in cheek—shared that the best way to estimate how long a project would take was to pick a number and times it by three! As it turned out that was a pretty useful method, never having estimated a project length before…

My interest in writing had previously given me experience with interviewing and research and in the first four days on the job I'd managed to accumulate copious notes. I had a fairly good idea of what sort of rota system they wanted, even if I didn't yet know what it was going to look like.

That weekend I set out to list everything I knew and thought they would need. I came up with a huge list. I then started digging deeper and working out what I'd have to code and build to develop the system.

As I did this, I started to work out how long I thought each component would take and began to build a Gantt chart showing when I would work on each component. (If you've not familiar with Gantt charts, they allow you to work out and show what needs to happen in a project, how long it's going to take and what order it all happens in.) I'd been introduced to the concepts of Extreme Programming and Agile development at College and was heavily influenced by the concepts of tackling high risk components first and developing tests at the start to ensure the components were developed in a way they would definitely work and I used this methodology to minimize risk to the client.

Over the course of that Easter weekend I produced an A2 sized Gantt chart detailing everything that I thought needed to be done. I had allowed extra time for components that I was uncertain of, plenty of time for testing and I estimated it would take me approximately three months to complete.

I wondered if I'd just wasted my weekend (which I wouldn't be paid for). Would I go into work on Tuesday, present my findings and estimate of three months' extra work and be told to clear my desk.

In some ways that might have been the preferable option. I was on a temp contract—not an IT contract. I'd gone down from a respectable £12 an hour to an okay £8 an hour and here I was proposing to extend that lower wage from three weeks to three months.

The job was complex, it was going to require a high degree of skill and knowledge—much of which I still had to gain. So maybe the low hourly rate wasn't such a bad deal after all. Weighing it up, it seemed like the perfect opportunity. I was willing to put in extra time and effort to complete the project. I was confident I could deliver what they were asking for due to the skills I'd learned in college, but could not show I'd done so previously. If they paid me less than an experienced professional would have asked and in return got the system required and I got some valuable experience it was a win-win situation.

However, I didn't feel all that confident walking into the office on Tuesday.

I must have presented well though as they signed off on my proposal, accepted my project plan and gave me the go ahead.

I then marshalled all my resources to make the project succeed. I got permission from the organization to write up the project for my final college dissertations, in part by suggesting that I would then be able to draw on advice from tutors if needed. I was able to ace both the Database Design and Human Computer Interface modules by doing this! I bought a wonderful book – Alison Balter's Mastering Microsoft Access 2000 Development which enabled me to get my head round database development concepts in Microsoft Access I still hadn't come across. I took problems home with me and did online research.

A month or so into the project I had to make a hard choice. I was offered an interview with another company. It was a long, fixed term contract paying far more than the £8 an hour I was getting. Did I take the interview and then possibly have to decide whether to abandon the project?

In the end I decided not to attend the interview. I had a sense this project was important for me. The project would end and jobs with higher wages would come along.

I think it was the right choice—at that time.

I met with challenges. My intention to tackle high risk components paid off when I found the organization's security was so locked down I couldn't use a planned Active X component (a piece of software used when programming in Microsoft languages). This meant I might not be able to deliver one of the core functionalities allowing users to view a complete rota for a week.

Fortunately, I found a workaround. Instead of a slick graphical interface I came up with a simple display of table data. Creating a temporary table that was populated on the fly with the data I wanted to show and displaying that data in a form that could easily be refreshed turned out to be just as effective.

At one point I was asked to accompany a manager when they visited a software company to discuss another project. In passing I was told that software company had also been asked to quote for the project I was doing. Their quote had been £30,000 to deliver similar functionality.

I was going to provide the functionality for £3,000…

I bit my tongue, kept my mouth shut, and filed that news away for later thought. The client got a bargain!

I completed the project by my new deadline and the organization was delighted with the result. I still look back on that as my gold standard of project delivery: completing a complex project with complicated algorithms allowing them to ensure EU working time directive was being taken into account on a 24/7 rota; and calculating pay depending on what time of day and what day of the week an individual was working. I provided a useful set of reports along with a detailed user guide and technical manual.

I felt able to now call myself a systems analyst—I was on my way!

The dreaded interview

By the time I left the role with the Crown Prosecution Service, I'd had a fair bit of experience of job interviews, some of which had led to offers and quite a few more that didn't lead anywhere.

Job interviews were a source of great frustration to me. I've always been fairly sure that if you show me what to do, I can pick it up and do a decent job, yet most interviewers seem only interested in what you've done, not what you are capable of.

My first ever job was arranged for me by my father. He told me to put on a shirt and tie, then took me down to the local hardware store and asked the proprietor if he had a job for me. The owner gave me a stern look and asked if I was a hard worker. There were a couple of other questions and comments designed to make it clear that he expected me to put some effort in and then he shook my hand and I had the job. It would, without a doubt, go on to be the easiest interview I would have for many years. Not that I understood that at the time.

Later on, I had an interview that was quite unusual. When we first moved to York, I saw an ad in the paper for people with Scottish accents. I couldn't believe that would be a valuable skill, but I phoned up and got the job.

They were looking for a Mystery Shopper. Someone to telephone car dealerships in Scotland, pretend to be interested in buying a car and test them on their customer service. I'd done some acting as a child and with my experience researching and writing, I was possibly overqualified.

I ended up not enjoying that short role as much as I thought I might. Being paid to deceive people wasn't something that sat comfortably with me. I got through most of the calls okay until I called one dealership and, right from the off, the man who answered was extremely suspicious. He kept questioning me and it seemed clear that he didn't believe I was who I claimed to be. Maybe my acting skills weren't as good as I'd thought…

When we decided we weren't moving back to Tajikistan I ramped up my efforts at applying for jobs. I suppose like most people, when looking for a new job I tend to focus on types of jobs I've done before, and companies that do similar things to those I've worked for in the past.

With the experience I'd had working for printers, one ad stood out, a salesman role working for a printing company. I've never considered myself to be a salesman, but when you are desperate for work sometimes you'll try anything.

This was my first two stage interview and having passed the first stage I was called back for a one to one interview. At one point I was asked to sell myself to the interviewer. I gave a poor answer that obviously showed I wasn't a natural salesman. Yet, he offered me the chance to have another go at answering the question. I thought for a minute and then made a much better effort at selling myself. I have no idea now what I came out with, but they offered me the job.

I turned them down. Despite needing work, despite having been able to dredge up some capacity for sales, I knew deep down that I was and am not a salesman. Work would have been a constant struggle and source of stress. In addition, the more I found out about the company, the less sure I was that I wanted to work for them. Their business model was publishing educational material to be placed in schools that was sponsored by local companies. The companies paid to advertise in the books that were printed which paid for their publication, my salary and the company's profits. I found myself questioning whether companies would really benefit from the advertising and how many adults would read the books.

It took me back to the times I'd fund raised in the past and I knew that I would have to have utter conviction in the benefits of the business to be able to "sell" it to others. I just didn't.

Because I had junior management experience from my time in the hospital laundry and leading a small team while abroad, I tried applying for a team manager position for a call centre. I was advised that there would be a role play as part of the interview. How do you prepare for that?

I had no idea. Turned out that I was completely unprepared for that interview. It possibly was the most disastrous interview I've ever attended. I left the premises thinking even less of my managerial capabilities than before.

The situation that threw me was when the interviewer played the part of one of my team members. It was revealed that they were thinking of leaving the company for a different job. My mind was blank in the short time I had to prepare for the role play scenario: a regular one to one with this employee.

I decided, based on my complete lack of knowledge of how to handle the situation, to reveal that I knew the employee was thinking of leaving and to ask what it would take to keep them in the company.

Big mistake.

I'm still not sure what the right way would be to handle that scenario, but that was definitely the wrong way. I wasn't offered the job. Interestingly, I found myself reliving this scenario in a future role, but more about that later...

I applied for a role at a small software company. I had an okay interview and then was told that they would like me to come in and work for the day, just to see if I was a good fit.

The fact was that my experience up to that point was limited. Not only my technical experience, but perhaps more importantly, my experience of working with clients and of job interviews.

At one point in the day I was taken into an office and sat down in front of a computer. I was told they had an online form that needed completing and they wanted to show me how to enter the data. That sounded fine. I'd worked in clerical roles before and was comfortable entering in data. Then they showed me the process.

If you imagine a computer form with easily over a hundred fields sized about the equivalent of two sheets of A4 paper sellotaped together to double height. Then imagine being told to enter data into two dozen fields at random positions dotted around those sheets with no discernible order to the process. Then try and remember the exact order you need to follow to correctly fill in the form.

I think I must have had half a dozen goes at it and could not work out a pattern I could follow. Each time I had to ask where to select next, I felt more and more embarrassed.

After the first or second attempt I should have said something like: "I'm going to stop you there. The fact is that it will not matter how many times you show me how to fill in this form, unless I have a clear set of written instructions, I'm not going to manage to do it. This form would benefit from redesign and it will both cut down on mistakes and speed up the process if we take the time to do that."

I should have said something like that. Instead my brain went into full-blown panic as I foolishly thought that if I couldn't do what they claimed was a simple process, that I would never get the job. I wonder now whether that was a test of my ability to recognise and challenge a broken process. Needless to say, I didn't get the job.

While working on the CPS project, I also interviewed for a bank based in West Yorkshire. They were using the JADE programming language for their systems and as I'd studied JADE at college, I applied.

The role would have required working a shift pattern to support branches in other countries and would have paid £18,000 once the shift allowance was taken into account.

I'd worked shift patterns before at the helicopter company over ten years previously and knew that while they can offer some perks, they are quite demanding. With a third child on the way, I wasn't sure I wanted to commit to being out of the house more than I needed to.

I was also beginning to understand that the skills I had developed at college and in the two contracts I had worked on were far more valuable even than I had been paid for. The realisation that the CPS had been quoted ten times as much as they had paid me for developing a software application had been quite an eye opener. If larger software companies can charge that much for their skills and expertise, was there room for me to charge a proportion, or even to match them?

In addition, I would either have had an hour and a half commute every morning and night or would have had to move closer to the bank. Neither option was appealing.

I was offered the role at the bank but turned it down. I then got the impression that they were insulted, as if they were offering me something I should have been grateful to accept. I wonder how many recruiting managers think that the jobs they advertise are ones that people should be grateful to be considered for? I wonder if more of us understood our potential if we'd be as happy to settle for what we are offered.

Freedom

I was job hunting while I worked on the CPS project, knowing the project would come to an end. There was very little IT work in York and it was looking more and more likely I'd have to commute. Where we stayed in York, we were concerned that the high school our kids would end up in had a poor reputation. We began wondering about moving back to Scotland as the Scottish central belt seemed to be prospering and the commute to Glasgow or Edinburgh was not that bad no matter where you were based. We found high schools in central locations that had excellent reviews.

I've found in the past and found this time that job hunting when you're not based in a location is almost impossible. I applied for jobs in Scotland but was not invited for interview.

I graduated from college in July, hiring a gown which seemed overkill for a Higher National Certificate, yet looking back I'm glad I did. Completing the college course was pivotal in my career. Had I not gone to college I may never have gone on to get a degree. I certainly would not have been offered my first IT contract.

My third child had been born only weeks earlier and we were once again in that place where time becomes fractured and days merge into nights. It didn't seem like the best of times to be making a life changing move, but we did it anyway.

Part of the reason was pure practicality. If we waited in York and I managed to get another short-term contract, we couldn't move till that was over. That would then put our move smack in the middle of the school year disrupting our older children's lives yet one more time.

As the central belt of Scotland seemed as busy as anywhere else in the country I had as much a chance of finding a job as by staying in York, potentially a greater chance of finding one without a long commute.

However, we chose to stay in Argyll, not exactly the centre of Scotland! The reason for that was purely practical, we could stay with family without having to give a timescale for when we'd be moving out. It did mean that I was again potentially looking at a major commute until we found somewhere more central.

I applied for local jobs wondering if we could just settle in Argyll. There were one or two possibilities, but my lack of experience in IT hampered me. The college course had allowed me to start winning contracts but the contracts I'd completed had been aimed at graduates, not at experienced developers or systems analysts.

However, I did have a couple of things going for me. My first contract was with Nestle, a well-known manufacturing firm. The second was with the Crown Prosecution Service. I had been blessed to get roles with respected organizations. I had delivered excellent work and had good references.

Also, I now had some experience in the most common programming and database development environments used by businesses around Britain: Microsoft Excel and Access.

I've found IT departments often shun and detest Excel and Access business applications seeing them as unsupportable burdens that cause far more problems than they care to deal with. Yet the business side of organizations sees them as vitally important tools that enable people to deliver fast solutions at a greatly reduced cost to that of an IT delivered solution. Time and again I've been able to deliver a solution at a tenth of the cost quoted by IT.

There are risks for businesses when they use Excel and Access solutions. While many of them do an excellent job of automating processes and simplifying work, there are solutions that are undocumented, poorly understood and vulnerable if the person who developed them leaves the company.

I see these as an opportunity. I and other professional developers can analyse and document these solutions, can train up staff to maintain and support them and give the business reassurance.

I got my next big opportunity working on a short-term contract doing just that with Microsoft Access databases. The company at that time was Alfred McAlpine. They were taken over a few years later and no longer exist as a separate company, but at the time they provided facilities management services: a fancy term for employing other people to change your light bulbs... and maintain your ventilation systems... and your automatic doors, etc. etc.

Alfred McAlpine had hundreds of engineers based around the country, each with a special (at the time) mobile device that could track their location, send them instructions and record their progress on a job. Many of our clients had agreed service level agreements with us and we had to be able to account for the length of time it took to respond to a request and how long it took to fix the issue.

Well over a dozen Microsoft Access databases had been developed to provide the reports managers needed. Each served a purpose and most managed data from more powerful databases. The developer had moved on and they urgently needed someone to help them ensure the processes could continue to run while also documenting how the databases were designed and how they worked.

The contract was again paying £12 an hour.

It was a tough role. We were always under tight deadlines with managers sometimes literally shouting for reports. I'd worked with engineers before at British International Helicopters, so it wasn't a shock to have people shouting in the office, but it hadn't made for the most effective working environment then and didn't now.

Some managers seem to think that shouting at a person to hurry up—or even giving them an unreasonable deadline—is a way to improve performance. It's not.

It takes much more skill and management capability to find what will positively motivate an individual and apply that but unfortunately there are bad managers just as there are good managers. In a few places I've seen colleagues crushed by that sort of overbearing management style.

Personally I respond well to recognition that a job has been done well. My default setting is loyalty. Once I commit to working for a company, for the time I am there, I work for them as if I'm working for myself. Actually, I tend to work even harder as they are the ones paying me!

I also respond well to a clear need, a defined goal, and most of all—achievable targets. I've had managers give me what they liked to call "stretch-targets". Targets that in theory require an employee to learn new skills, to find ways to become more efficient and productive. I certainly aspire to learn new skills and be more efficient and productive, however I know from painful experience that increasing efficiency and productivity is sometimes only possible by working increasing amounts of unpaid overtime. When employees learn new skills this may benefit an organization in the long term, but in the short term either productivity goes down or training has to be done after hours for no immediate reward.

Occasional "stretch-targets" where the benefit to both the organization and employee is clear can be useful motivators, but I've seen them misused and employees punished when they fail to meet targets that stretched an employee beyond what was possible, or possibly even worse when they meet the targets and are then "punished" with new and ever more demanding "stretch-targets".

Some managers consider failing to meet targets they have imposed on employees to be the employees fault. However, this is a short sighted view that takes no account of the effect on a person's long term loyalty to the company, their motivation to continue putting in extra hours, or their desire to go above and beyond what is expected.

It's maybe worth saying that I've had managerial responsibilities in several roles. I've sat at the other side of the recruiting table. I've had to discipline employees. I've had to set goals and targets. I've had to find ways to motivate and inspire my team. I'm writing this book for employees and those who work for themselves and most of my experience has been as someone who worked for others and depended on them for pay increases or promotions. I'm also writing from the perspective of someone who currently works for themselves though ultimately depending on others to pay for work done.

Despite a sometimes strained working environment I was delighted when I was offered a permanent role at Alfred McAlpine. This meant we could apply for a mortgage, find our own place and begin to settle our family.

We ended up choosing to live in Cumbernauld, one of Scotland's "New Towns" in the Scottish Central Belt with train lines and buses direct into Glasgow and a short journey away for the Croy train that goes to Edinburgh.

I went from a short-term contract paying £12 an hour to a fixed salary of £20,000. From where I was only a few years ago, I had again doubled my salary.

But I wasn't content.

Prior to my move into IT I'd never worked for a company or organization for more than three years. My average was a year and a half. I'm a drifter, a nomad. Partly circumstantial. I could blame my parents who uprooted me at age six and then again at age eight and maybe there is some truth in that.

I wanted to marry and that meant moving once and then again two years later when my wife got her first "proper" job. (I emphasize proper as she'd taken a degree that required three six-month work placements during the four years. This meant she left university with a year and a half's experience and that experience was as valuable to many employers as her degree!)

We uprooted everything to go to Tajikistan but then had to leave it all behind for uncertainty when the danger became too great.

We moved to Scotland to increase the chance of us both finding work. As well as IT roles for myself, my wife's degree and experience are in Analytical Chemistry. The central belt of Scotland is the nation's industrial heartland and there are a fair few opportunities not too far away.

I've been coping with change since early childhood and if I don't get some every now and then I worry I'm going stale.

And I have to confess I'm also a dreamer. I believe in taking chances, in giving up something allegedly secure for something exciting. I have left a role to pursue my childhood ambition to write. In part, this book is a fulfilment of that ambition, an acknowledgment that my heart's desire is to put words on paper and hopefully tell a story that someone else might enjoy or find useful.

Things came to a head when, after a year at Alfred McAlpine, we had our pay review. I was called into a meeting with a senior manager and told that my salary would be increased by £700.

Not having stuck around in most organizations for long enough to have my salary reviewed it was a shock to be presented with a pay increase that essentially meant I was treading water. Most people experience inflation at a higher rate than what the Government states and the media trundles out.

Doing the maths, that £700 equated to a 3.5% increase on my salary. If I stuck around in that role for any length of time, I would be able to keep paying my bills, but would never be able to save for the long term future.

We had applied for Tax Credits (if I remember correctly) as far back as 2003. The thousands of pounds we received then was a life saver at the time, but it was also a complicit acknowledgment that we were unable to earn enough as a family to provide for ourselves. The Government were telling us—you are too poor to provide for yourselves!

Despite my now permanent salary and 3.5% increase, we still were receiving thousands of pounds in Tax Credits each year.

How could it be right that I as an individual was doing what the company considered to be an important job, yet my pay was not enough to take us above the Government's definition of poverty?

I wrote a proposal for a higher increase, but this was not accepted. Then I started looking for a new job.

Perhaps some employers would see this as a sign of disloyalty, or perhaps some employers wouldn't want to employ someone who is willing to jump ship if they don't get the pay they demand.

From my perspective, I was trying to get a handle on how I could improve my financial situation and I was unwilling to accept that someone else could tell me what my lot is in life, that I had no choice or say in the matter. I was perfectly willing to remain loyal to Alfred McAlpine; however I was beginning to understand that my own loyalty might not be rewarded and that the only person who had the power to decide what salary I could earn was myself.

Summary

Consider your long term future. What do you want to be doing when you are fifty, sixty years old?

There is a training course with your name on it, suited to you.

You are responsible for your own learning, for the rest of your life.

Experience is cumulative. No-one can take away from you what you have already learned.

Many skills you can learn can be used in many contexts.

To win a contract or gain a promotion, you may have to put in many hours of unpaid work.

Understand who you are, what you are skilled at and what you have no talent for, and use this knowledge to direct your career.

Make every effort to build good relationships and gain good references. These will be invaluable as you present yourself to a new client or employer.

Make an effort to learn how to use common software programs like Microsoft Excel and Access. Spreadsheets and databases offer enormous potential to simplify work processes.

If you can develop a process to consistently save an employer time and money each day or week, or to consistently earn more money, you can justify your value based on the cumulative effect of that change.

The only person who has the power to decide what salary you can earn is yourself.

Prompts and suggestions:

Do you know what you don't know?

Are you willing to seek out what you need to know?

How do you feel about going back to school, signing up for a training course, or going to college or university?

How long have you been in your present role or situation?

Would you still like to be in your present role or situation in five years' time?

Have you ever learned how to manage a project?

How do you prepare for interviews?

Have you ever taken training for interviewing technique?

Have you ever worked out how much you are worth to an employer or client?

The third time I doubled my salary

Put it in the bank

With the expansion of the Internet it was becoming easier to find work. Job sites like S1Jobs.com, Monster.com, and Reed.co.uk allowed me to upload my CV and companies—including recruitment agencies—could search these great online databases and find me.

Early in 2007 I got a call from one agency asking if I'd be interested in a role with Barclays Wealth. Having recently had my first experience of a pay review and on being told Barclays were offering a starting salary of £23,000, I absolutely was!

It was my first experience of being head hunted and it wasn't to be the last. The Internet has made employee loyalty a much more important issue for companies. My CV is online and searchable 24/7 to anyone—for a small fee—in the world. LinkedIn.com took a different route to the above job sites, creating a business networking site that allows me to make my CV available to everyone for free. Potential recruiters still need to pay to get contact details, but in my view LinkedIn.com has become the number one web site for anyone interested in career progression. The ability to include references from former employers and colleagues embedded within the CV adds authenticity. Instead of just squeezing a couple of lines about relevant interests to round out our character, we can upload photos, video, and presentations. If you've developed your own training materials or 'how to' guides, you can share samples. And on top of that are the connections you can establish that allow search algorithms to link you to people with similar skill sets and experience, making it easier for recruiters to find you.

All this means that if someone needs the skills and experience I have, there is much more chance they are going to call or email me, which means that I have to do far less work sending out CVs and applying for roles. That being said, it hasn't stopped the need for me to work at finding work and there are times when I find myself back job hunting, applying for relevant roles in addition to responding to agency interest.

So, back to Barclays. I was recruited to a permanent role with a starting salary of £23,000. This was an 11% increase on my salary at Alfred McAlpine. The thought did occur to me that maybe switching jobs was a way to guarantee increasing my salary beyond inflation. However, I didn't yet want to believe that.

I left on good terms with my former colleagues and manager, as I've done in every role I've left. There is no point in letting any issue prevent the possibility of having a working relationship in the future.

I was full of hope for the role at Barclays. They sold the role as having unlimited potential to do well. Barclays had an excellent bonus scheme in place which could pay up to 40% of an individual's salary. The bank was doing well, they had ambitious growth plans, this seemed like a place I could allow my ambition to thrive.

It only took a year for that ambition to die.

I enjoyed my time at Barclays, but there were a couple of things I could not get my head around. The growth targets were one of them. At regular meetings we would receive reminders of the plan and expectation for growth. Barclays had managed double digit growth for the past three years and projected the same level of growth for at least three years into the future.

Despite my best efforts, I just could not believe it. An individual can increase their work output by double digits, can even in extreme cases up output by 100% over a short period (though in that case you have to question how much time they were wasting before!), but to sustain that for three years and then expect that increase to continue… No, that just didn't seem possible.

Of course, Barclays did not expect us all to increase our performance to that extent, no, at least some of that growth was to come from expansion. Barclays intended to grow itself by merging with and acquiring other companies.

Only a month after I started, Barclays announced it was bidding to acquire the Dutch bank ABN Amro, a £46 Billion offer that would have propelled Barclays to become one of the top five banks in the world.

Barclays pursued the ABN Amro acquisition with fervour. Working for the bank at that time I got the sense that we were going to win the race, that nothing was going to stand in our way. But then, at the last hurdle, The Royal Bank of Scotland won the bid.

It was shocking to me, as a very junior member of the company who had been fed confident progress reports on the acquisition for months. At the time it seemed like a disaster for our company, a blow to confidence. We were not the number one bank we were portraying ourselves to be.

However, it was only as the financial crisis revealed itself that I began to understand the real disaster would have been if Barclays had won the bid and taken on so much bad debt.

Ten years on and it is worth exploring those events a bit further. Success can easily breed pride and lead us to have a blinkered view of ourselves. I know that my ambition has caused me to pursue wealth and a higher income in ways that have not been as honourable as I would have liked. I've tried gambling with stocks and shares and very nearly lost a lot of money that I couldn't afford to lose, all because I was more concerned with short term gain over long term character.

I believe the senior Management of Barclays became so focused on their ambition for growth that they stopped asking whether growth was the right thing to pursue, that they failed to carry out the due diligence required over such a large acquisition. If you've ever seen the 2015 movie: The Big

Short, it sums up perfectly what was wrong and maybe still is wrong with our financial institutions.

Back to late 2007. I was just a cog in a very large wheel and the ABN Amro debacle was not ultimately a big concern for me. I was, as every employee was, given regular updates on progress but had nothing to do with the deal. No, instead I was solely focused on my own small corner of that empire and finding that yet again, I couldn't get a handle on what I needed to do to progress.

Bonuses were a huge issue. Those that had worked for Barclays for years occasionally talked about them and for some there was an undercurrent of resentment about the way bonuses were distributed.

Your own contribution played a large part, but you were also judged as part of a team and part of a department. There was even rumoured to be a bell curve distribution where only a few people got the highest bonuses while others had to make do with the crumbs that were left.

If a bell curve method was being used to determine bonus payout I believe that would have been patently unfair and far more likely to damage staff morale than improve it. But it was only a rumour. How the bonuses were agreed and distributed was a closely guarded secret. A black art that we Proles could only guess at.

I tried to get a handle on what I needed to do to maximise my bonus. I was highly motivated and wanted 40%. I plagued my manager with questions, but even he could not give me the answers I was looking for.

Quite simply, I wanted to know what was expected of me and how much I would need to up my game in order to achieve the highest bonus. It was a simple equation. I was willing to put the effort in but wanted some assurance that there would be a payoff at the end.

I was influenced very heavily by my experience at York College where I'd been told exactly how to earn a distinction in each module and could see how much effort I needed in order to succeed.

At Barclays I wasn't able to get the guidance or assurance I needed.

In addition, we kept getting changing messages about our priorities as a team. We would be told to focus on one area, only to be redirected to a different one before the first priority was fully resolved. This raised concern that our bonuses were in jeopardy. Although we were following instructions from on high, we were also at risk of being penalised for following those same instructions since we could not demonstrate a clear improvement in one area. Yet, if we refused to switch priorities, we would be penalised for doing so. It was a lose/lose scenario.

In the end I did receive an excellent bonus for that first year: 20% of my annual salary, but I was only to be graded at band C. I confess that before I thanked my manager, I grilled him with a series of questions as I tried to find out what I could have done differently. Perhaps I was just too impatient. I was told that it was rare for anyone to get higher than band C in their first year. However, that was just a red rag to a bull. If it was rare, that implied that it was possible to get a higher band. Perhaps I was being too literal, something I still struggle with. Did rare actually mean never?

Over the next few days we held whispered discussions as a team. Had we been judged as a team and department? Had the shifting priorities held us back? Had the bell curve been applied and held our bonus down?

I didn't and still don't know. However, I knew that I was not willing to live with the uncertainty. If I couldn't know how much effort I needed to put in to receive a certain result, then I wasn't willing to sacrifice time with my family for that uncertain result.

I updated my online CV.

My ideal salary

I inherited three thousand pounds in 2008, money that I could spend any way I wanted. I decided we needed a holiday. I took my family to France that summer and was on a train heading for Euro Disney when I got a call on my mobile. Was I interested in a contract position?

My experience of the annual performance review at Barclays had disillusioned me, just as it had at Alfred McAlpine. Without clarity on how I could improve my performance I was uncertain what future I had at the company.

I'd had long discussions with my manager, with colleagues and had also been researching online. Ultimately, I concluded that I had two options within Barclays, either I could progress within the organization by climbing the career ladder—moving into management—or by moving departments. It was only through a change in role that I could progress.

This was incredibly frustrating. I liked my role, I was good at it and I could see how I could expand my skills to make myself even more useful. Yet that wasn't valued within the Barclays structure as much as I valued it.

My only other option was to move out of the company; I could progress by finding a better paying job.

It was a harsh lesson in reality: I was solely responsible for my career.

Partly out of a continuing desire to show an improved performance and somehow, possibly gain a higher bonus, I was doing more work. I was travelling to Peterborough every other month to manage the transfer of business processes to Glasgow. I was becoming responsible for those processes which potentially could double my workload. It was too much. There was no way I could physically double my workload without working a shed-load of unpaid overtime and that I was not willing to do—especially when there was no guarantee it would be recognised at bonus time.

But I had to make some effort to improve the situation. So, on one of those trips down to Peterborough, I started working on an idea that had been building in my head.

I was by now quite advanced in both Microsoft Excel and Access development. I was a competent VBA programmer and experienced database designer. I had noted that most organizations chose to only install the basic Microsoft Office suite as a cost saving exercise. If people only need Word, Excel and Outlook why spend an extra £100-£200 per person in an organization of thousands of people to give them the professional version of Office which includes Access?

But the Access database software was extremely useful. By storing data in a database rather than in a spreadsheet, it could be far more useful and accessible. So why not use Excel as the front end to an application and use Access as the database? This would allow users who only had Excel to still read and write to an Access database sitting on a shared network drive. A whole department could access the same data simultaneously without the issues they had sharing Excel spreadsheets, which often became corrupted when multiple users tried to edit them at the same time.

I had created a front and back end Access database system at the Crown Prosecution Service, a system where each user had their own copy of a database containing forms for viewing and editing data along with reports, and a single back end database to store the data. I was confident I could create a similar database system using Excel as the front end.

My biggest stress at the time was Business As Usual (BAU), supporting hundreds of Excel processes that existed throughout the organization. I was unable to clear the backlog and I knew that there must be a better way of managing the issues that arose.

I decided, on my own initiative, working evenings and weekends, to design a support call system that would allow me to better manage those calls. This was to be my first Excel/Access system and it proved to be a huge success.

My manager was somewhat taken aback when I showed him. I had gone ahead and developed a completely new system without any authorisation.

I had hoped I could fully track what I was doing and demonstrate the need for a new member of the team. It didn't work as I expected. By implementing the system I managed to bring down the backlog far faster than I thought possible. As a result, I also was not able to show that I was spending more time than I had available.

The root problem had been that I didn't have a workable system to manage the support issues. As soon as I developed one, a large portion of the problem went away!

The system was such a success that I was then allowed to go on and use the concept to develop an improved system for a different team. That little project gave me my first experience of training hundreds of users to use a system, an incredibly useful experience.

While we were bringing up the business processes from Peterborough, we did have an indication we would also get extra resource to support them. Following discussions about career progression I then was given a chance to manage that resource.

I did what any self-respecting geek does in that situation, I went out and bought a book: Managing for Dummies! It was great and gave useful, practical advice that I could follow.

On the flip side though, it gave me insight into the responsibilities and capabilities of management. This combined with previous experience managing teams made me even more uncertain about the best way to progress my career.

While I'm good at managing myself, I'm not a natural manager of other people. I'm able to manage projects over which I have a high degree of control, or of the parts of projects where I have that degree of control. I can manage people and have managed people, but it is not the career path I felt suited to pursue.

I was doing a lot of research around that time, reading up on opinions and articles on management and career progression. I came across one article online that I now regret not keeping. The article suggested that there is a breakdown in relationship that happens when an employee tells the employer they are looking for a new job and is extended when an employee is offered a new job.

The author of the article suggested that both the employee and employer need to think very carefully about what to do when an employee is thinking about leaving. (Remember that role-playing interview I'd had some years previously…)

If an employee is thinking about leaving, what is the motivation? There is a high likelihood that salary is a consideration in which case if that employee is valuable it may make sense to offer a salary increase to motivate the employee to stay. But how long will that last?

Will the employee develop itchy feet in another year and the employer yet again have to consider what value that employee is to the company? How long can that continue? This can be exacerbated if the employee gets into their head that the best way to get a salary increase is to threaten to leave!

Salary is only one motivation for changing jobs. Employees move jobs for many reasons, sometimes even reasons they are unable to express, even to themselves. There may be several reasons, some obvious, some below the surface. While an employer has the right to ask why, they have no right to the answers.

Many of you reading this will have left jobs yourself. I couldn't begin to guess at all the reasons you will have had. Along with positive reasons for leaving such as an increased salary, better working conditions, more satisfying work, many of us may also have had negative reasons for leaving a job. It is rare that an employee will want to discuss those negative reasons for fear it will burn their bridges with that company or result in a bad reference.

After that call on the Paris train I was faced with this scenario. Did I use this opportunity to demand a higher salary or did I cut loose and run? The contract was intriguing—six months with Sun Microsystems, a company I held in high esteem for their gift to the world of the Java programming language and the MySQL database: both freely available. The contract was at a daily rate of £190 a day. I didn't know the hourly breakdown at that point, but at seven hours a day that would have been £27.14 an hour!

I did the maths. If I worked for 44 weeks at that rate I would be earning £41,800 a year! This was the chance to achieve my third goal!

My manager was disappointed when I told him I'd been offered the role and was considering taking it. I did not want to try and bluff my way to a higher salary. I could see that if I did, the expectation on me would simply be raised and the only likely route would be a managerial one which I did not want to pursue. I explained most of the reasons I was leaving, the increase in income (though it was not guaranteed long term) and the opportunity to work with one of the world's leading technology companies. I didn't discuss my disillusionment with the long term aims of Barclays as a company or frustration at being able to understand how I could progress longer term.

A senior manager was called in to discuss the situation. I suspect, though this was never confirmed, that I could have had my salary increased to £30,000. With a 33% bonus that could also have taken me to £40,000 a year but that could not be guaranteed. I was also giving up my pension, but I saw no reason to explain why that was no incentive to me whatsoever.

In the end we parted on good terms and I still regularly meet up with my old manager. I think that for me it was the right thing to do. I doubt I would have stuck long at Barclays had I stayed and they increased my salary. I had too much knowledge of how things worked by that point to believe that a permanent role was the right path for me.

Sunshine

Leaving Barclays for Sun Microsystems was not an easy decision. There was something otherworldly about the whole recruitment experience. I had a telephone interview initially with one manager based in the UK and another based in the US, both calling into the conference call with me. The call was slightly stilted with none of us being able to read body cues. I decided early on that I needed to take control of the call and began offering information and asking my own questions to spark a discussion, my writing/interviewing skills again proving valuable. At one point I was told the contract was for an initial three months, not the six months I'd been told by the agency.

I didn't question this during that initial interview but did have words with the agency afterwards. It's a common issue for contractors. The available funding gets squeezed and the message is not communicated. Suddenly being able to earn in six months what I'd recently earned in a year was not looking so likely…

That telephone interview must have gone well as it led to a face to face interview in Linlithgow. I found myself adopting a relaxed attitude from the start, even taking off my suit jacket as I walked into the interview room to match the more relaxed formal wear of my interviewers. I had taken a notepad into the room and as soon as the interview started began to take notes. I've found this helps me to remember key points and can prove invaluable on the first day when that interview is otherwise long forgotten.

I don't remember many questions. Essentially, in my idealised memory of that interview it seemed to boil down to one simple question: can you do the job? Yes, I told them confidently, I can.

I had done my preparation though. I'd learned from some valuable experience when applying to Barclays. The

Barclays interview was the first one where the agency provided me with a step by step guide on how to excel at interviews. The Barclays interview process was competency based using the STAR method. (Situation, Task, Action, Result) I'll go into this in more detail later, but basically it works as a prompt to answer questions, allowing you to demonstrate your skills and knowledge in a relevant way.

That agency also advised me to be familiar with the company and after all I'd learned from Barclays about company structures and stocks and shares, I researched Sun Microsystems all the way down to the annual revenue and current share price. I had also researched the software I'd be working with. Sun owned StarOffice, a competing office suite to Microsoft Office. You could program in Visual Basic though the syntax was different. While Microsoft Office claimed to be Object Oriented, StarOffice was far closer to that goal, being quite similar to Java. It was suddenly helpful to be able to mention those two OU courses I'd studied…

The interview seemed to go well and on the way out I found myself chatting to the manager I had previously spoken with on the phone and we seemed to get on.

I had, they offered me the job.

When your projected income from a role drops from £20,000 to £10,000, should you cut and run? I'd taken the opportunity during the face to face interview to bring up the question of why I'd initially been told the role was for six months. They explained that the funding had only been agreed for three months instead of the six that had been asked for, but that they expected there would be work and funding ultimately for six months. In the end I decided I would take the risk and trust the funding would come through.

I think one of those managers later told me he had checked out the online profiles of the interviewees. It was the first confession I'd heard that this practice was used to further vet people. It made me think: what electronic signature am I leaving out there for other people to find. While I don't think my Facebook account shows anything out of the ordinary, I've since made an effort to restrict access to what I post. I see no point in having a prospective employer decline me for a job just because we vote for different political parties or because I've confessed that I don't much care for their football team.

By the way—I'm an independent voter who has voted for five different political parties over the last twenty years. I've not been impressed with any of them and, if possible, I won't be voting for any of them ever again. Also, I'd much rather be playing football than watching it...

Sun Microsystems fostered an environment that encouraged creativity, rewarded initiative and trusted people. I couldn't believe at first how different it was to almost every other company I'd ever worked for.

From day one I was encouraged to work from home. I was given complete leeway to redesign the spreadsheet they were using as a pilot system. So, I did as any self-respecting developer does, I got on with it.

Within a week of examining that spreadsheet I had over twenty questions. I arranged a meet with one of the hiring managers. I've always got some reticence about asking questions. Does it make me look stupid if I don't know something or can't figure it out myself? Part of that thinking is learned behaviour. Teachers who indeed called me stupid for asking questions that seemed obvious to them. Also, managers and colleagues who were too impatient.

I didn't get any of that at Sun, instead the manager was delighted I'd done such an in-depth analysis and helped me as much as he could.

My career choice of systems analysis/developer has meant I will always be asking questions. I'll always be risking working for someone who doesn't understand and looks at me askew, but that's okay. I now make sure that if ever I'm asked in an interview how do I tackle something new that I include saying I'll ask colleagues or my manager as well as doing my own research. If a company doesn't want employees who ask questions, then I probably don't want to work for them anyway.

The design of that initial pilot spreadsheet was impressive. It had been created quickly to resolve a need to provide reporting and took data in from two sources and summarized it to enable automatic emailing to managers. It had achieved that initial task perfectly. However, as with many rushed projects there had not been time to document the process or to put it through load testing.

The main problem they had with it was that as the project had grown, the spreadsheet had been taking longer and longer to run the automatic process. By the time I started, it was taking four hours. The guy who was running it wasn't even able to use his computer, it required so much processing power.

My first priority, after analysis, was to find a way to speed it up. I immediately turned to the online forums. Google was my friend. I was aware that in Microsoft Excel there are a couple of coding tricks you can use to speed up operations. These are fairly simple lines of code that reduce the amount of work a spreadsheet has to do.

I often find that although many people use spreadsheets, few understand how they work, so forgive me if you already know this. Spreadsheets are wonderful tools for making quick calculations. Because it is so easy to write a formula and see the result, then to change the values and immediately see the difference, spreadsheets have become essential to many companies. Changes to one cell in a spreadsheet can literally affect every other cell, sometimes millions of formulas might need to be recalculated on-the-fly.

But, that recalculation has a cost. Each one takes time to run and multiplied by the complexity of the formula and the number of formulas that exist on the spreadsheet, well, it didn't take me long to realise that the spreadsheet I was working on was trapped in a kind of loop. Automated changes were being made to cells, pulling in new values. Every single time a cell was changed, every other cell on the spreadsheet was being recalculated!

Yet, that recalculation only needed to happen once: after all the cells had been updated. I added a line of code to stop the spreadsheet calculating automatically before the values were being updated, then a second to turn on calculation once it was safe to do so, and a third line to force the recalculation to take place. Three lines of code and I reduced the time taken for the process by some 75%.

Another issue is that when the recalculation takes place a similar problem occurs with the screen being updated every time a formula recalculates. That meant the screen was being refreshed thousands of times taking up more computer processing time. That also only needed to happen once. Another two lines of code and I was able to bring the running time of the process from four hours to under half an hour. Over the next weeks I restructured the code to remove unnecessary routines and further speed up the process. Eventually it was running in ten minutes.

I kept on working to fully document the code changes and to refactor the code to make it easier to read, adding comments and formatting. In the end, for myself as a programmer, it was a thing of beauty.

My contract drew to a close and I was offered the chance to move into one of their reporting teams, supporting the project to convert the pilot into an online reporting tool. Suddenly I was being given the chance to gain experience with development and support of an Oracle data warehouse and Oracle's Business Intelligence software.

I saw this as a fantastic opportunity to expand my experience to a different brand of reporting software which would hopefully make me more employable in the future.

I worked for that team until Oracle ultimately bought out Sun in February 2010. Most of us contractors were laid off at that point. I was given one month's notice and so my CV now has a very short length of contract with Oracle.

Sun Microsystems was one of my favourite jobs— right up there with the buzz of working for a helicopter company and the childhood dream of the chocolate factory. The level of trust, the openness, and the opportunities I had at Sun were all wonderful. I was sad to leave.

But I was a contractor and one thing most contractors end up doing is leaving. So, after almost five years of continuous employment and after it became clear the contract market had dried up, I headed down to the Job Centre to sign on while I continued looking for work. Now that was a soul-destroying experience.

When the well dries up

I was brought up to believe we have a responsibility to work and earn, and believe there is a deep need inside men to provide for their family. When I haven't been able to do this, I've found it soul destroying. At school we were shown an episode of Boys from the Blackstuff. A TV drama series about five unemployed men in the late seventies. I'll never forget the character Yosser Hughes ambushing people with the demand "Gizza' job!" At times I've felt like making the same demand when I've tried all I can think of to get a job, only to be constantly turned back.

Back in the mid-nineties, when I'd previously signed on, I'd had interviews where I was guided towards applying for jobs that I had previous experience in or that matched my skills. That made some sense, but was frustratingly limiting. I knew that I could develop new skills, that I was capable of trying new roles. In 2010 I quickly found myself asking why I was being required to jump through the same hoops.

By that time, I'd had so many jobs, sat in so many interviews—from both sides of the table—and applied for hundreds more roles, that I already knew far more about what I needed to do than the polite people who had to interview me at the Job Centre every fortnight.

Before I signed on, I'd already created a spreadsheet I could print out and take with me that listed the companies I had applied to, the job titles applied for, the contacts at the agencies I'd sent my CV to, the telephone numbers, the email addresses… It was a wealth of information and each week I was adding between five and ten new roles as I found them.

I took the opportunity to use the Job Centre's new computer system and gave up pretty quickly. It was dire. No ability to search key words, no ability to store a search and have results emailed daily. It appeared to have been designed by a committee that had never had to look for work themselves.

My experiences of signing on for unemployment benefit in 2010 made me realise that government is incapable of finding me a job. Perhaps if they stopped giving those interviews and instead spent time training anyone who lacks job finding skills, we'd have less people out of work. Even better, if the Government actually supported industry instead of allowing it all to be sold off to other countries, we might still have an economy. Rant over.

My experience at Sun of using Oracle software was useful in getting my next contract at Edinburgh University. Just a short four and half months, but at an even better daily rate: £250 per day! Do the maths… At seven hours a day that was £35.71 an hour! If I worked for 44 weeks at that rate, I would be earning £55,000 a year!

The only problem was the job market had continued to contract and had almost completely dried up. By the time that contract ended I was only able to get one interview and then didn't get the job. I kept searching for work but there was almost nothing out there and I had dozens or hundreds of contractors all competing with me for each role.

I was soon back at the Job Centre, but we had been saving hard. All the extra money that had been coming in had been squirreled away. I signed on for a couple of weeks and then gave up and signed off. I'd saved so much money in the previous few months they weren't likely to pay me.

Instead it made sense to use the time to try and get the Creative Writing course and with it my degree through the Open University completed. If I could get ahead on that I'd not have to spend as many evenings and weekends when I finally did get a job. I also thought I could finish my novel though it turned out I'm not very good at writing one piece of writing while editing another.

I loved the course though. It gave me exposure to forms of writing like poetry and auto-biography that I wouldn't normally have chosen to study. It shouldn't have surprised me that I enjoyed poetry so much. I love music and every song that's ever been written is basically a poem set to music. Auto-biography is another area of writing that surprised me by how much I enjoyed it. I think in large part that is down to the number of job interviews I've had. At some point I started to enjoy telling people about my life...

Earning a degree

When I first wrote down my Three Goals, I had no real idea how to achieve two of them. Earning a degree on the other hand was fairly simple. You either enrolled at university and worked hard for three years or could work part-time for a longer period.

The maths was simple. I had four years to get a degree. A university degree is based on achieving a certain number of credits. Divide that number by four and I would need to complete enough courses with those credits each year to get that number.

While at college we'd been asked if we were interested in going on to study a degree. York College was wondering about expanding its role to offer foundation degrees. We were told that our HNC would count towards all or part of the first year of a university degree. I was already part way there!

I applied for a credit transfer with the Open University and did indeed get the full first year credit: 120 points. A standard degree without honours is only 300 credits so I only needed 180 to go, or 240 credits if I wanted an honours degree.

Like brick and mortar universities, OU courses each count for a different number of credits, the standard being 30 while tougher courses can give you 60 credits.

You need 120 credits of level two courses towards your second year and at least 60 credits at level three for your final year for a basic degree, or 120 at level three for an honours degree.

In 2007, while still at Alfred McAlpine, I signed up for my first level two distance learning degree course which would give me 30 credits: M255 Object-oriented programming with Java. I completed this in 2007 and the following year tackled the related course: M256 Software development with Java which gave me an additional 30 credits. I was half way through my second year of university and a year and a half into my goal journey.

I then had a gap while my wife went back to university herself and we decided that two parents shutting themselves away every weekend might just destroy our family.

When I'd started looking into OU courses I was intrigued by the Computing degree that included systems courses. I still considered Systems Analysis to be my core discipline and reading the review, I could see how the systems course: T306 Managing complexity: a systems approach, would be useful in terms of learning how to manage complex projects and understand the complexities that beset every organization.

In 2009 I received an email stating the OU was planning to discontinue the systems courses. I still hadn't completed all the required credits at level two, but I was desperate to achieve the level three systems course T306 which seemed the most interesting of the two. Completing this would give me a full 60 credits at level three. I signed on and had my world expanded as I learned to look at the world through a systems lens.

I was due to complete T306 in 2010 which gave me another two years until my fortieth birthday. By this point, as a family, we were exhausted having had either myself or my wife studying almost constantly for three years. I didn't know how long I could keep going for at the same pace.

I now only needed 60 credits at level two to complete my degree and had pretty much given up the thought of continuing on for an honours degree by this point. While the level three 60 credit course had required more study than the level two 30 credit courses, it hadn't been double the workload and the courses took the same length of time. I knew it would take me longer and more work to tackle two additional 30 credit courses.

I kept looking at the IT courses, but none of them seemed to offer both 60 credits and a subject that I really wanted to do. So, I started looking at other disciplines. A215 Creative Writing had amazing reviews. Dozens of people raving about how good it had been. Then I found that the course had no exam! I was sold.

I'd done very well in my course work for the previous OU courses but didn't fare as well in the exams. I had an average of 98% for my first set of OU assignments, but still could only get an overall grade two pass because my exam grade took me down.

However, even though I only managed a grade two pass in my final exam for T306, this was the first exam in my life I actually enjoyed. My preparation went well and I sat in that exam room pouring out my thoughts and opinions, my pen hardly stopping for the full three hours.

Creative Writing then proved to be the absolutely right course at the right time. My first goal had been to write a novel and I had indeed been slowly working towards that.

In 2009 I was reading 100 Ways To Motivate Yourself and was inspired by one of those suggestions to start work on a novel that had been burning itself into my soul. The suggestion was deceptively simple and combined a couple of the ideas from that book:

Do something every day towards a goal. Work out what the target is. Divide the target by the number of days to achieve the target. Do that amount of work each day and you'll achieve your goal by the target deadline.

I wanted to write a 100,000 word novel and so I reasoned that if I wrote 25,000 words a year for four years, I'd only need to write 100 words a day, five days a week. If I wanted to complete that novel in two years, I'd only have to double up my word count.

But I faced the same problem that some new writers face, I was trying to achieve too complex a story without having the skills to manage it. I couldn't reconcile the multiple plot lines I wanted to include in my novel Fallen Warriors. The project grew out of my control and after writing 60,000 words I eventually had to shelve it.

But our tutor in Creative Writing introduced us to National Novel Writing Month, #NaNoWriMo. A free to enter "competition" that has no judges and no prizes, just the satisfaction of completing a novel. This marvellous event occurs every November and a year after I'd completed the required number of courses for my OU degree, I took part and completed my own first 50,000 word novel. Just a few months before my fortieth birthday I'd achieved two of my Three Goals!

The final chapter

Our savings were again running out when in early 2011 I got a call from an agency. I have to say this is one aspect of online life I love—people calling me asking if I'd be interested in a job!

The agency was recruiting for a fixed term role at HarperCollins Publishers. Nine months paying a pro-rata rate based on £40,000 a year.

After five months being out of work I jumped at the opportunity. And, while it wasn't for a full year, it did allow me to be earning my target salary. It was a come down from a potential £55,000 a year, but for contractors, potential is pie in the sky anyway, we have to earn a lot while we're working and save as much as we can, because five months of nothing can come along at any time.

HarperCollins was another of those wonderful opportunities that I wouldn't have had if I'd taken the safe route as a permanent employee. I was fortunate to work with another great team and for a manager who taught me a lot.

Strangely enough, working for a publisher, I also got the opportunity to read a lot. I was able to introduce my kids to The Hunger Games series before it became big and also discovered Game Of Thrones which I'd completely missed when it first was broadcast.

As it turned out, the project over-ran and I ended up working at HarperCollins for over a year. Remember that pro-rata salary… I finally achieved the third of my three life changing goals: earning £40,000 a year at the age of forty!

I was head hunted again as the project at HarperCollins drew to a close. I had to decide whether to hang on for another month after the project had already gone live, as I would have had less and less work to do.

I chose to leave. The memory of five months unable to find work was fresh in my mind and I really did not want to risk waiting only to find the job market had dried up again.

But I also had a decision to make. Contractors in the UK, especially IT contractors, are either required to set up their own limited company and provide their own liability and indemnity insurance, or to sign up with what is called an "umbrella company", which deals with all the insurance and other legal aspects on your behalf. One clear benefit from either option is the ability to reduce one's tax bill, though the limited company route offered more possibilities than an umbrella company.

I'd used umbrella companies for several of my contracts in the past and wondered if this was the time to set up my own company.

So, what are the benefits of either option?

With an umbrella company you become the employee of the umbrella company. The client or agency pays your fees to the umbrella company who charge you a weekly or monthly fee. I was paying a monthly fee of £75 in 2010 to the umbrella company. Your normal place of work is assumed to be your home office and so all mileage, travel costs to the clients site and other legitimate expenses can be claimed and used to reduce your tax bill. The umbrella company then works out your PAYE Income Tax and National Insurance contributions after these expenses have been taken into account. I found that each month, the reduction in tax ended up covering my monthly fee and more.

With a limited company you become the director of that company. You could in theory then pay yourself under the threshold for Income Tax and National Insurance and instead take profits from the company in the form of dividends which traditionally was taxed at a lower rate than Income Tax and National Insurance. The company has to pay for all relevant insurances, accountancy fees and other legal costs which normal employees don't have to consider, and of course any profits are taxable under corporation tax. Accountancy and other expenses can easily reach £1,000-£2,000 annually depending on your line of work and whether you take the cheapest options or not.

In 2012 when I had to make this decision, the benefits of creating a limited company were a lot clearer. Unlike income tax which increased to 40% for taxable income over £34,370, corporation tax for small companies was 20% all the way up to £300,000. Back then dividends were taxed at a nominal 10%, but the government then did some fancy footwork to return that using a tax credit. If you were likely to earn even a few thousand pounds over the higher rate threshold it made a lot of sense back then to set up your own limited company. I certainly hoped to earn more and decided it was time to set up my own business.

In 2009 I expanded on my original list of Three Goals when I took up a challenge to write down 100 goals. In thinking about what I wanted to do and why, I ended up looking at this list of 100 goals and the thirty first goal I'd written stood out to me: To be and do all that God wants of me.

I didn't want my career to be solely focused on money and decided that, while I wanted to enjoy the benefits of having my own limited company, I also wanted to do so in as ethical a way as I possibly could. I decided to call my company Goal 31 Ltd. I would not use my ability as a company director to avoid paying National Insurance or Income Tax, though would limit the amount of those taxes I paid, knowing I would pay Corporation Tax on company profits and enjoy the legal option of paying myself a dividend out of the remaining profits. Given the furore in recent years about off-shoring of people's income in order to evade tax, that's a decision I'm really glad of.

Summary

Use online job and business networking sites like LinkedIn.com, S1Jobs.com, Monster.com, and Reed.co.uk to share your CV and allow recruiters to find you.

You can learn the skills to develop systems and processes that will make your job easier to do and make you more valuable to your employer or clients.

Books can be a relatively cheap way to expand your knowledge. Libraries are free. Many books are now available in audio format if you don't enjoy reading.

Interviews are your chance to sell yourself to an employer or client. Make the experience as easy as possible for them by being prepared and being willing to take the lead if you get the sense the interviewer is struggling.

Be willing to ask questions, as many as it takes when you start a new role. If you do it in the right way, this shows your eagerness to learn and desire to gain competence. It is far better to ask questions in the first weeks, than later when you should have already learned basic information.

Sometimes you need to refine a process again and again, otherwise it may not be able to cope as volume of work increases.

The State or Government are not responsible for providing you with work, only you are. You can develop the skills and knowledge you need to find your ideal career.

Always save. Put money aside for a time when you might be out of work. You'll be glad you did.

Higher level educational courses and technical courses can be a valuable investment, giving you skills and knowledge you can use immediately, and insight into questions you need to ask to enable you to progress your career.

There are tax advantages, along with risks, to setting up your own company.

Prompts and suggestions:

Have you created an online CV?

Which job and business networking sites have you uploaded your CV to?

What are you doing to look now for your next job?

What could you do to make your job easier?

What processes do you have to do that could be made more efficient?

How would you make them more efficient?

If it meant doing some unpaid overtime to make your job easier, would you do it?

Have you researched what books are available in your local library that could improve your knowledge in your ideal career?

Have you looked at further education courses to see whether these could help your career?

Are you doing something every day that can help develop your skills or complete a project?

Could you afford to save, even a small amount, each week?

Would you consider working for yourself?

How to double your salary

The obstacles we face

I've shared how I doubled my salary three times from the age of 16 to 40. I want in the rest of this book to try and draw out some advice that might help you to do the same or even better.

The fact is there were three fairly short periods of years during that time where decisions I'd made seemed to contribute to my being able to earn more. I've doubled my salary by following simple advice that is available to everyone and yet I don't see everyone working towards the same goal. So, if this advice is already available to everyone, why doesn't everyone try to double their salary? For that matter, is it even possible for everyone to double their salary? To the first question I believe there are at least six obstacles people face:

1. Some people are trapped believing they are unable to dramatically change their circumstances.
2. Some people don't know what other people earn and so are unable to realise they could earn more.
3. Some people have poor role models.
4. Some people lack the knowledge they need to improve themselves.
5. Some people have never had the support network of good parents, wider family, communities or friends to direct them and to teach them and encourage them.
6. And it must be said… Some people choose to be lazy.

I've had to deal with some of these obstacles and I know people who are trapped by one or more of the other obstacles. If you are facing any of these obstacles, they may seem impossible to overcome, but just realising an obstacle exists actually starts to empower you to overcome it. If you've read this far, you are already better prepared to overcome each of these obstacles than you were before.

But I want to address the second question first. Is it truly possible for everyone to double their salary? Well, I would argue that my first job was at minimum wage: £2 an hour back in 1988. I don't think there was a concept of minimum wage back then, certainly not an official one, but I was certainly at the bottom of the wage ladder. In my lifetime, I would argue that anyone in a similar role earning the same as me has already seen their wage almost doubling twice over. In 2019 as I write this, anyone in work aged over 25 is now entitled to receive at least the official minimum wage which is £8.21 an hour. If you were earning minimum wage like me back in 1988 and are still earning the same wage now, your income has almost doubled twice whether you worked for it or not.

If you have never tried to earn more than minimum wage, imagine what you could achieve if you really tried!

As a child I read Robinson Crusoe and found myself fascinated by the simple arithmetic of a man planting seed and reaping a harvest, hundreds and even thousands of times what he sowed. If you've got a garden, access to an allotment, or even a window sill that gets sunlight, I encourage you to try planting some peas and sunflowers in early spring. Water them daily and put some canes in the soil to tie them up as they grow.

It is an amazing sight to see the first buds appear, then a growing stalk, and on pea plants, the flowers appear. One pea can result in anywhere from five to twenty pods growing. Each pod can contain anywhere from two to ten peas. You can obtain two hundred peas for the one you planted. Sunflowers on the other hand only produce the one flower, but that flower can contain hundreds of seeds! Planted outside, the seeds might produce such a crop without any effort from you. This world we live in is designed to enable us to prosper. If you are willing to work hard, to learn, to try, then many things will be possible for you, even doubling your salary.

But let's take a closer look at the list of obstacles above starting with the one that's both the easiest and the hardest to deal with:

Laziness

Laziness is a choice and everyone can choose to not be lazy. Whether we do so or not is entirely up to us and that's why it's both the easiest and hardest obstacle to overcome. If you just can't be bothered making an effort, if you would rather watch TV or sleep or do something to entertain yourself rather than actually work, then nothing I or anyone can do will help you. You are on your own.

But you don't have to be. Try and make an effort. Choose to learn something. Choose to develop a skill. Go to your library and read. Sign up to a group. Get out of your house and exercise.

Laziness is a habit and if it is a habit you've developed, you will only be able to break that habit by replacing it with the habit of working.

Being Trapped

Why do people believe they cannot change their circumstances? Back in the late nineties I was trapped in this belief myself. I believed I had failed at school and so wasn't capable of going on to receive further education. Because I was rejected for better paying jobs, I believed I was only able to apply for lower paid work. You may have different beliefs that are holding you down. Perhaps what others have said or are saying about you, perhaps you believe your lack of resources prevents you from making changes, possibly you compare yourself to others and think you could never achieve what they have achieved.

My beliefs above were not based on truth. It took time for me to stop believing those lies about myself.

In primary school, I had a teacher that I respected. One day I was messing about, I can't remember what I was doing, but he felt I required a special lesson. He called me out to the front of the class and made me repeat, three times: "I am stupid."

I didn't believe that statement, yet I also, for well over a decade, absolutely believed it. I knew I wasn't stupid, but something about that experience held me back for years afterwards. Eventually I realised that I had to forgive the teacher. And so, for weeks, any time I recalled the incident, I consciously forgave him. I didn't become any less stupid, because I wasn't stupid to begin with. I had been messing about, probably. I can't even remember what I'd done or was supposed to have done. Forgiving him released something about that incident that previously had held me back. It's no accident that soon after forgiving him, I went on to sign up for my first higher education college course.

Back in 2003 we had little savings and were still receiving Tax Credits and financial support from family and friends. Because our resources were so little, I was able to receive a grant towards my college education. Sometimes our lack of resources can allow us to access funding that the better off cannot. The following year, my wife having had a regular job and with my contract work, it turned out that I wasn't eligible for the same grant towards college fees. In just a year, our resources had increased.

I've often been guilty of comparing myself to others. It's a dangerous habit. Chances are that there will always be other people more successful in some way than we are, but their success does not lessen the value of what we are able to achieve. If you are going to compare yourself to anyone, compare yourself to who you were last year. If you haven't changed in any way, haven't improved your life in some regard, do something about that so that next year you'll be able to look back and be able to say I'm different to who I was.

If you have been trapped by your beliefs, then I hope that by reading this book you will start to find freedom to overcome this obstacle. There are very few circumstances where we cannot choose to improve our lives. If you still don't believe that your situation can be improved then I encourage you to read, watch or listen to stories of other people who have managed to make dramatic changes to their lives. John Kirkby's story in the book Nevertheless was one I found especially inspiring. I can also highly recommend the film: The Pursuit of Happyness which tells the story of Chris Gardner.

No knowledge of what others earn

You've worked for your employer for ten years. Your salary has barely gone up with inflation. You're getting by, but only just. Other people seem to be able to afford to live in nice houses, drive fancy cars and take holidays, but not you. Why is that? Do they really earn more than you? If so, how much more?

There are many resources that allow you to find out what other people earn. This book is one of them. I've tried to be honest about my own earnings over the years in order to show what is possible. Also, I want to share a useful tool that allows you a great deal of insight into what thousands of wigwam type entrepreneurs earn. It's not free, not totally, but it's easy enough to access and costs very little. What is this useful tool? Companies House WebCheck service. The UK government enables you to search more than 2 million companies and for as little as £1, you can download a company's annual accounts:

www.gov.uk/government/organisations/companies-house

If you want to know what my earning potential has been since I founded my company Goal 31 Ltd in 2012, all you have to do is log onto Companies House and download the accounts I've submitted each year. I'm the only employee in my company so whatever my revenue was on those accounts, that's what I brought into the company during that year. It's not been a straight line up, but it is trending in a direction I'm happy with.

Of course, that's not the only place you can look. The Office of National Statistics produce comprehensive reports on earnings. I've only scratched the surface, but if you want to know what other people earn, you can start searching here:

www.ons.gov.uk/employmentandlabourmarket/peopleinwork/earningsandworkinghours

Job adverts can be a great source of information on what people are earning. Not every advert will contain salary or day rate details, but a fair number do. And if you look online at the job boards, you can search by salary or day rate ranges to find out what jobs are available in your ideal salary range!

Check out:

www.s1jobs.com
www.monster.com
www.reed.co.uk

There are many others as well, just run a search for job sites…

It can be a lot harder to find out what people are currently earning within a company. Organisations have a vested interest in protecting this information. Personally, I feel that is a mistake, but it is reality in many organisations. There is nothing to stop you asking HR what the salary band is for a particular role…

Poor role models

Why does it matter whether we have good role models? We have a tendency to copy what we see others do. You might understand this as peer pressure, but it is also part of an inner desire to belong to community, to be accepted. If we see people around us working hard then there is a sometimes subconscious pressure on us to conform and to also work hard. If we see those around us lounging about, we'll want to join them.

There are many potential role models in life. Our parents, family members, teachers, coaches, friends, neighbours, colleagues, employers, and even complete strangers can act as our role models for good or bad. Obviously, I know nothing about your childhood or your current situation, but if you had no good role models in the past, that doesn't mean you can't develop role models now.

Writing this passage, I did an online search: "how to find role models" and found several useful articles on different sites. A couple of these are listed below.

How Women (and Men) Can Find Role Models When None Are Obvious (Wendy Murphy 01 Jun 2016) hbr.org/2016/06/how-women-and-men-can-find-role-models-when-none-are-obvious

How to Find an Inspiring Role Model (Nozomi Morgan 14 Nov 2016)
www.huffingtonpost.com/nozomi-morgan/how-to-find-an-inspiring-_b_12917502.html

I've been blessed to have good role models around me my whole life. I almost take it for granted that I can find people to inspire me and challenge me. The major reason for this is that my parents took me to church. Even though we had several major moves during my childhood, I could always be sure that each Sunday, we would go to church.

What impact did this have? From an early age I was taught that before God, everyone is equal, that we all have flaws. I was taught that humility is better than pride, that serving is something we should all aspire to and the best leaders are those who serve others. I was taught that hard work is rewarded and laziness results in poverty. I was taught that we all are given skills and abilities and we should make every effort to use these to benefit God and others. And I saw that those people in the many churches we attended who applied these lessons to their own lives often prospered. Not everyone, and not always financially. Some of the most content were those who didn't have as much.

No matter where you are, there will be good role models not too far away. You just have to decide to look for them. Local business owners are often great role models. Shopkeepers, bakers, cafe owners, they often start working early in the morning and after their shop is closed will be working cleaning and tidying and readying for tomorrow.

You walk into town and see someone jogging. How many people around you are choosing to go out for a run every day, timing themselves, measuring the distance and challenging themselves to go faster and further.

Your local library will have many biographies of successful people. If you want to find out what they did, the obstacles they faced and how they overcame them, all you have to do is read.

Before I move on it's worth stating that nobody is perfect. If we have found someone we look up to, who is skilled or experienced and whom we would like to learn from, it can be devastating to find they have flaws. It is vital to realise that we can still learn from excellence and genius while choosing to reject other aspects of a person's character or actions.

Lacking knowledge

Back when I turned thirty, recently returned from working abroad and feeling like an utter failure, I realised that I didn't know what I needed to know. I knew I was being held back, except no-one else was holding me back, it was only myself. Other people around me seemed to know what to do, seemed to have plans and purpose while my future seemed like a fog.

Admitting to myself that I didn't know what I needed to know was a prod to start finding out. For me the direction I took was to sign up for further education. That might help you, but there are other ways.

Some people seek an apprenticeship, to learn from someone or a group of people with greater experience and skill and knowledge.

Some people launch straight into a new venture with an attitude that they will figure things out on the way. Failure is a great teacher. Something doesn't work, we can learn from that and use our God given abilities to come up with different ideas.

Whether you choose education, apprenticeship, learning as you go, or a combination of all three, you can discover questions you didn't know you needed to ask and answers that will help you make better decisions.

Lack of support network

If you don't feel you have anyone around you that can offer support, please understand that you will never build a support network around you if all you do is take. There needs to be a willingness to give on all sides for a support network to really function. You may well have to give before you can receive.

There are many different types of support networks. I mentioned how I've found many good role models in the churches I've attended and it's there that I've also found the best support network. Examples of other good support networks are business networks. I'm a member of the British Computer Society and in many cities members of the BCS will meet monthly giving an opportunity for them to swap advice, to network and meet potential new clients and partners.

My company is also a member of the Federation of Small Businesses and they also offer many similar networking opportunities.

There are hundreds of groups, associations and organizations in the UK for many different types of businesses and skill groups. There may be several relevant to you and the direction you want your career to take in the area you live. In addition, there are thousands of such groups available online worldwide. They don't offer the same in person, face to face networking that a local group offers, but can still be useful in making contacts and sharing advice.

If there isn't an existing network or association in your area for the type of career you are pursuing, why not start one!

There may be other obstacles you face that effectively put a "Do not pass" sign right in front of you. There may be occasions where you need to choose a different route to end up in the same destination. At other times, you may need to choose a new destination. Recognising reality is not admitting defeat, but always remember that most obstacles can be overcome with determination and effort and a willingness to change.

Pyramids versus Wigwams

In today's world you really only have two types of career structures: pyramids or wigwams.

All medium and large companies have a pyramid career structure. You have an ultimate boss at the top of the pyramid, perhaps a board of directors or senior partners, then one or more layers of managers before reaching the workers at the bottom.

To progress in terms of earning a higher salary, often the only way is to take on management responsibility and work your way up the pyramid. Except, each upwards layer is narrower, often extremely narrower than the one before. Each manager may have ten to thirty staff reporting to them. Management roles may not become vacant very often and in applying for those you are not only competing with dozens or hundreds of colleagues, but hundreds or thousands of external applicants!

Some companies and organisations are better at rewarding workers than others, and some roles within the organisation are better paid than others. But there are usually limits. To stand a real chance of increasing your salary within a traditional pyramid structured organisation, you may well have to move roles, teams or even to a different company altogether.

Pyramids by their nature don't move about, and those who work for them tend to adapt to being stationery. Wigwams on the other hand are designed to be taken down and moved on whenever needed.

I consider anyone who works for themselves to be using a wigwam career structure: flexible, adaptable, willing to take on new clients and roles and challenges.

Small companies may also fall into this category, family firms where almost everyone is on an equal footing, sharing in the profits together; partnerships, entrepreneurs, even some forward-thinking small businesses where they've realised that when people are paid equally, they are more likely to take ownership and responsibility.

In a wigwam structured company, the only limit to your success is your imagination and willingness to work.

Every large organisation and company in the world started off with a wigwam structure. One or two or three people who built something so successful they had to employ more people to help them. They didn't start off with layers, but unfortunately many companies seem to have developed them with all the limits on creativity and ownership and responsibility that accompanies them.

I heard someone talking about the eighty/twenty rule again recently. Eighty percent of the work being done by twenty percent of the people. If this is happening it implies that eighty percent of employees are being carried by the twenty percent who are doing the bulk of the work. In a large organisation, it's easy to hide.

If you are one of those twenty percent, it's hard to make others aware that you are the poor individual doing the eighty percent of your team's work!

When larger organisations can recognise who is actually contributing the most to the company's success and profits, it's possible to reward those people appropriately. This is much easier in a smaller, wigwam type of company where it's usually obvious who is pulling their weight and who is not.

What do you need to double your salary?

You either already have the basics of what you need to double your salary, or you can develop a foundation to build on. In some respects it's not that complicated:

- Character
- Presentable
- A good work ethic
- Skills
- Knowledge
- Interview technique

Character

Your character is the foundation which determines how successful you will be in life. Are you honest? Do you act with integrity? Do you treat others as you would like to be treated? Do you have a positive attitude? Are you friendly? Are you assertive?

It certainly is possible to double your salary dishonestly, to bully and manipulate your way to earning more, but if that is the path you choose, you will never be a success. There will always be a risk that your dishonesty will be found out, that someone you have bullied will turn on you and undermine what you have.

It may take slightly longer to build good relationships, and earn the respect of others, but in the long term those relationships will be invaluable in your career.

Presentable

Turning up at your place of work in unwashed, torn or inappropriate clothes, and with body odour discouraging people from approaching you may not hold you back if your skills and knowledge is such that a company has no choice but to ignore how you look and smell. But why would you make it harder for people to respect you if you want to improve your chances of earning more?

Personal hygiene should be a given. However, we've created a culture where it's difficult to be honest with each other. Thirty years ago, if you'd turned up literally stinking, your boss would have either had a quiet or not so quiet word with you and you would either have dealt with the hygiene issue or been shown the door. Now people are too scared of being sued to be honest with each other. I'm not saying you should only smell of the latest aftershave or perfume. If I've had to run from the train to the office because my train was delayed, I sweat. But I also wash daily and use deodorant which are basics of good hygiene and make it less likely that sweating will adversely affect body odour.

Many companies have dress codes. It's worth reading them and following them. You may not be able to afford the most expensive suit, but it costs very little to shower daily, use deodorant, brush your teeth, and buy presentable clothes.

A good work ethic

Your work ethic is determined by your character. If you are not willing to treat others in the way you want to be treated, if you are not willing to take ownership of someone else's problem and determine to resolve it, your work ethic will be undermined. Work ethic is not just about working hard, though that is a part of it, it is about accepting responsibility, about caring, desiring to have done the best job you could.

A good work ethic is based on seeing all the work you do as working for yourself and desiring that you perform to the best of your ability. Your ability may not currently be that of an expert or professional, but if you are performing to the best of your ability now, that is all anyone can ask of you.

It is not all you should ask of yourself though. A good work ethic is constantly inspiring us to learn more, to develop our skills, to understand why things are done, and question if there is a better way.

Skills and Knowledge

I decided to combine these two for reasons I'll get to in a minute… Starting with skills, some people specialize, others develop a broad range of skills. I tend towards the jack-of-all-trades end of that spectrum.

Even if you know what career you want to pursue, it's not always obvious what are the most important skills you need to earn a higher salary. Some people seem to get by with remarkably little skill… Others are underpaid to a sickening degree.

It will certainly be easier to develop skills that you have a natural ability in. If you know what you are good at, taking training or finding ways to stretch your ability in those skills will allow you to progress faster than in areas where you are not naturally talented.

I'm not a football fan, but even I can see there are many football players who might not be able to bend it like Beckham, but earn a very good income by using their natural talents.

I know of children who won't even bother trying to develop their skill in football because they didn't start young enough and they are already so far behind in competency. Perhaps they are right to realise they may never make it to the Premier League, but I feel the attitude that "I've missed the boat" is a dangerous one. When I decided to pursue a career in IT in 2003 you could have argued that I had missed the most opportune time. We'd just had a huge boom and bust with the millennium bug and the initial wave of dot coms. Everyone was a lot more wary of IT contractors and rates had plummeted. I had nothing going for me. I was in my thirties and competing with the cool young coders fresh out of Uni. I should have just given up and become a plumber.

Wrong!

I was perfectly placed to profit from pursuing this career even though I was yet to develop most of my skills. Although I didn't realise it at the time, I already had one of the most important foundations for a career in IT: knowledge of how businesses and organisations operate.

All those throw away lines on my CV gave me insight into retail, manufacturing, health, the Civil Service, aviation, stock control, how processes operate, what it's like to work in an office, on a production line. Whether you realise it or not, you also have knowledge based on your experiences that may one day be useful. Even if you are just starting out, your interactions with other people in non-work situations have given you some insight, if you're willing to learn from them.

Knowledge and skill are two different things, yet they are closely related. Anyone who develops any skill will also increase their knowledge. Skill without knowledge is a dangerous thing. Would you like to be operated on by a doctor who was skilled in wielding a scalpel, but had little knowledge of human anatomy? Sometimes you can only develop your skills by taking time to study and learn.

If you have a natural talent for cooking and would like to develop a career you have a number of options. You could apprentice in kitchens for cafes or hotels or restaurants, gaining knowledge and skills from those you work alongside. You could start by studying at college, learning basic food hygiene and theory. You could practise at home, testing your ideas on family, friends, and neighbours. You could specialize developing skills and increasing your knowledge in baking, meat, fish, vegetables, and confectionery. Skilled chefs are highly sought after and, as everyone everywhere needs to eat, if it interests you, there are opportunities to travel around the world.

Perhaps you have an interest in joinery. People have been working wood for as long as we can remember and many people start developing their skills by becoming an apprentice. You can learn almost all you need to know in many areas of life just by listening and observing and practising. But you will increase your knowledge faster if you make an effort to study and you have opportunity to expand your potential skills. If you only learn by listening and observing those around you, you miss out on the opportunity to learn from those who you would never get the chance to meet.

You can earn a good living as a skilled joiner, but there are a range of specialisations. Perhaps you tend more to the artistic and would want to develop skill in carving and sculpture. Perhaps you have more of an engineering or architectural bent and want to focus on construction—some amazing buildings have been constructed solely from timber. Then there is manufacturing—Ikea has made a fortune by simplifying manufacture using timber. There are unlikely to be any skills that will not benefit from improving one's knowledge.

Learning what others have done and how they did it. Learning from the mistakes of others. Learning the science, understanding the theory of how we interact and are influenced by what we do. It all informs how we use and develop our skills.

If you have existing skills and knowledge, they may not seem directly relevant to your chosen career, but even the fact you have developed skills or obtained knowledge shows you can do so in another field. And like I did, you may find they will eventually prove valuable, complementing your new skills and knowledge.

Interview Technique

Regardless of whether you intend to apply for other jobs, remain working for your current employer, or even work for yourself, it is vital to develop your interview technique. Interviews are mainly about persuading someone that you are the right person for a role and if you want to progress within an organisation or win a new client, the same techniques are necessary.

Be prepared. If you know what role you want to pursue, you may get an opportunity to impress someone who can assist sooner than you think. You may have heard of the term elevator pitch. The concept is simply that occasionally you get a minute to sell your idea to someone, about how long it takes when that someone is trapped in an elevator with you. If you're not prepared to use those few seconds well, you may never get another chance. Say you have set your sights on being promoted. Having a good knowledge of the responsibilities the position holder would have, of the "customers" the position supports and their needs, of the issues faced and suggestions for how you would go about dealing with them would all allow you to develop and practise a short speech showing how you would be the right person to be given the position.

First impressions matter in an interview, if only because your own confidence can be raised or squashed depending on how you feel you handled the first few minutes. However, every day is a chance to make a new first impression if you are already working. "Today is a new day." "I am going to work hard and excel today." "I care about my customers." All affirmations you can tell yourself each morning and strive to work by throughout the day. I can guarantee that if you have not been living by these principles and start daily applying them, your colleagues and managers will notice. It may not have an immediate effect, but if you consistently show an improved attitude, a positive outlook, your manager will be far more likely to listen if you ask for or enquire about promotion opportunities.

How other people perceive you determines whether or not you will get good references. This is where everything comes together to either lift you up or hold you back. We can only work with what we have; however if we start to improve, from that point onwards we can benefit from the effort we put in.

I've discussed the importance of being presentable above and don't want to rehash that. If you never wear a suit apart from attending interviews, will you feel comfortable when you walk into that interview room wearing one? It is always a good idea to practise an interview beforehand and a dress-rehearsal may well be needed if you are planning to wear clothes you've just bought. A suit, shirt, tie and shoes should not be uncomfortable to wear. It should be possible to buy smart looking clothes that don't strangle you, at a reasonable price.

Remember, interviews are a two-way situation. You will be judged on how you look, what you say and how you act, but you are also being given an opportunity to judge a potential employer. I still get nervous in interviews, still sometimes feel desperate knowing that I haven't worked in a while or really wanting a particular role. Regardless of this, the edge is taken off because I know that I am also there to interview them. Personally, I find it helpful to take out an A4 pad and pen alongside my CV. I've usually printed out a summary of notes that I took when researching the company and the role and also questions that I would like to ask. Questions along the lines of: "What will be my immediate priorities in the role?", "Could you give me some background to the project I'll be working on?", "Who will be affected by the work I will be doing?" or "Who will I be working for?" If you can develop the attitude that this is your interview, that you are in control of it, that can help you to squash your nerves.

If you turn up to a new interview or meet a new client dressed well, acting professionally, listening, engaging, asking questions and offering suggestions that show you understand the need, you've already gone a long way to demonstrating to the employer or client that you are the right person for the role.

You will probably find you need to improve in one or more areas before you can start to earn more unless you are currently underpaid for your skills and knowledge. Demonstrating professionalism in each of the above areas is a basic requirement if you want to double your salary.

Privilege

After I'd written the first draft of this book I was introduced to the cartoon: On a plate, a short story about privilege. You can read it here:

www.boredpanda.com/privilege-explanation-comic-strip-on-a-plate-toby-morris/

When I returned to working on this book, I knew I had to mention it because it is a challenge to the message of this book: that you can double your salary.

The fact is that I have been privileged. I came from a stable family where my father didn't run off leaving my mother to fend for herself. Both my parents were hard working and while there wasn't all that much pressure on me to do well at school, there was an expectation that I would help the family in practical ways.

My childhood wasn't easy. We moved twice while I was still young and losing friends and being the new kid was tough. I suffered from asthma which sometimes kept me bedridden. But my parents were able to ensure I was treated by the NHS doctor for my asthma and they had time to spend with me and my sister, food was always on our table and all of which and more meant I knew I was loved.

I was also privileged to be taken weekly to church meetings. I was introduced at a young age to philosophy and logic and ethics through those meetings, something that even today some university students miss out on.

I was taught that we were created by a God who loves us. That there is a plan and a purpose for my life and for everyone. I consider it a privilege to have had such a positive influence in my life through Christian teaching.

It has been a worry that whatever success I've had in my life might be solely down to the privilege I've enjoyed. If so, what value does a book like this have? If you haven't had the same privilege as me, does that mean you can never achieve the same? Of course not. There absolutely is some truth to saying that people who enjoy privilege have more opportunities, but having opportunities and taking advantage of them is not a given.

There are many people who are currently more successful in different areas than I am, who had less privilege than I did growing up. There are also many who had more privilege than I did who have not achieved as much.

It will be harder for anyone who has less opportunity and support. Yet many people choose to overcome the obstacles of their past and go on to tremendous success. I am convinced that if more people were aware of what is possible, more would seek to improve their situation and would find that they can.

I have no intention of apologising for the blessings I have received, instead I am thankful and grateful for them. It is because of these blessings that I've felt able to take the steps I've taken, that I've had the confidence to take risks. When you've heard the story of the prodigal son repeated several times a year for most of your life, and you have a family who will take you in if it all goes wrong, how much easier it is to take leaps of faith.

If you have had a privileged upbringing, like me, then you may need little encouragement to pursue your dreams. If not, then I hope you believe me when I say that many of your dreams are obtainable. It is possible for you to double your salary and more. It may take more effort, it might take more time, but then again, it might not. You are an incredible human being, created in the image of an incredible and awesome God. Each of us can do amazing things if we will only believe and persevere.

How my salary doubled

I would love to say it is easy to double your salary. If you just look at how my salary has doubled, perhaps you could be forgiven for thinking that wasn't so hard. Here's how my salary doubled:

	Salary
Shop Assistant	£4,000
Storeman (Base salary)	£8,000
Systems Analyst	£20,000
Business Analyst	£40,000

Of course, that list of figures leaves an awful lot out. Let's look at how long it took between doubling:

	Salary	Year	Time Taken
Shop Assistant	£4,000	1989	
Storeman (Base salary)	£8,000	1991	2 years
Systems Analyst	£20,000	2006	15 years
Business Analyst	£40,000	2012	6 years

While it was only two years to double my salary the first time, it took fifteen years to double the second time! The third time was a bit faster at six years and I was actively trying to double my salary for most of that time.

Maybe if you look at the number of years between each doubling above you might be tempted to say: If you are earning peanuts it is very easy to double your income. Yet that first doubling came at a cost. Remember I chose to reduce my income in order to receive training. I had no guarantee of a job at the end of it and no assurance that I was going to end up earning more.

It may have taken me fifteen years to then double my income a second time, but then, I didn't even have that as a goal back then! It was only in 2003 that I seriously began to try carving out a career. Then, as I focused on the goal of developing a career, that's when I began to gradually encounter opportunities that ultimately led to my doubling my salary a second and then a third time.

At no time though was there a quick fix. Each progression came at the cost of years of study, of hard work, of persevering even when it wasn't clear what the outcome would be. Through it all, I was always trying to find my purpose, to find meaning in my work.

Your ideal career

What is your ideal career? In many ways this is a far more important question than what is your ideal salary. What if you could do a job that you loved, that made you excited to get out of bed in the morning and allowed you to go home feeling satisfied that you'd achieved something? Would that be more important to you than a serious pay increase?

I hope so. Yet it is quite possible that finding and focusing on your ideal career will make it far more likely that you can double your salary. A person who enjoys their job, who is motivated to succeed, who goes to work each day looking forward to the challenge—that person is far more likely to invite success than someone who isn't sure they are in the right job for them. But how do you find out what your ideal career is?

In some ways I've been fortunate to have had a variety of roles when I was younger. Roles that allowed me to find out things I enjoyed doing and was good at, along with things I disliked and was clearly unsuited for. Yet I still remember the frustration of thinking everything was happening so slowly. Of wondering whether I was wasting my time in dead end jobs.

If you are uncertain what your ideal career would look like, how can you plan for your future? If you have no real ambitions or ideas to pursue, how can you set goals?

It is not the purpose of this book to help you find out what you should be doing with your life. There are plenty of other guides that will help you determine that, if you don't already know. However...

On 27 March 2003, having decided that we were not returning to Tajikistan, I visited Future Prospects in York and completed a computerised career matching survey. I was asked to answer dozens of questions and then received a printout of suggested careers.

The top match was Journalist which fitted in quite well with my dream of being a writer. Second match was Computer Systems Analyst. I had no idea what that meant other than something to do with computers…

Of the 22 matches the computer felt were "Very Good", eleven were computer or IT related, three were related to printing, and four were skilled or ordinary trades.

Would you believe the computer also included Beautician in that list?

I'm not sure exactly what I answered to bring that up. There couldn't be a relation to that career and another match: Spray Painter (Vehicle) could there? Or maybe it was some combination of an interest in art and talking with people.

If you are able to take advantage of a similar computerised system or online questionnaire, I highly recommend it. By the end of 2003, having completed a relevant module at college, I'd confirmed to myself that Computer Systems Analyst was indeed a career I wanted to pursue. You can find a number of websites that will offer career matching for free simply by using a search engine and searching using one of the following questions:

- What career am I suited for?
- What is my ideal career?

However, if you don't have ready access to a computer, and even if you do, you can also make some useful progress yourself simply by trying the following exercise:

Take a blank sheet of paper and write down everything you enjoy doing. Leave nothing out, no matter how irrelevant it might seem. If you enjoy gardening, knitting, spending time with your children, collating papers, playing Call Of Duty, cooking, five-aside football sessions, write all these things down, whether work or leisure related.

Then, once you've finished, rewrite out the list on a separate sheet of paper, grouping the activities. You may need to do this more than once as you see different ways of grouping them. For example, say you wrote down the following:

- Gardening
- Going on long walks
- DIY

You could group these together in several different ways:

- Working outdoors
- Physical activity

Also, Gardening and DIY could be grouped under Creative Work or under Tradesman.

You may not find your ideal career jumps out at you while doing this exercise, but that's okay; it wasn't obvious to me the first few times I tried. The main aim is to understand yourself better.

A useful follow-up exercise is to then write down all the things you definitely don't enjoy doing! For me that list would include:

- Selling
- Marketing
- Keeping Business Accounts

Unfortunately, these three activities are absolutely essential to every business I could want to run! At a very basic level, I need to sell myself or my skills; I need to market myself to potential clients; and everyone who wants to succeed in business should have a basic understanding of business accounts. Fortunately, we don't have to enjoy these skills to learn them and it is possible to begin to enjoy some activities once we take the time to develop them as a skill.

But, while I might need to (and indeed have had to) develop some skills in these areas, I know that these are not ideal careers for me. I would be miserable if I was stuck in a sales or marketing role.

If you are looking for ideas for possible careers, it would make sense to find out what jobs are available and what other people currently do. Sometimes hearing about other careers can help us realise we have an interest in that area. In the UK, the government has a National Careers Service and they offer an online database of job profiles:

nationalcareersservice.direct.gov.uk/job-profiles/home

Each profile explains:

- The skills and qualifications needed to get into that job
- What the work would be like
- The pay you could expect
- What the career prospects are

If you are not based in the UK, it is possible your government or even an employment agency offers a similar service.

It is one thing to imagine you might enjoy a career as a beautician, but what if you were to quit your current job only to find out you hated your new career? It is definitely worth finding ways to try out something before making life changing decisions. You may find your local college offers night classes. Taking a night class for a year is far less disruptive to your life than quitting the job that is paying your bills. Volunteering for an organisation at a weekend or one day a week may also allow you to test the waters.

At some point though you may need to accept a level of risk, knowing that it might not work out. Only you can decide if that risk is worth it. However, it will be valuable to talk the decision through with family and friends. You may also be able to receive careers advice directly and can talk with recruitment agencies to discuss whether there is a market for what you want to do.

Searching for your ideal job

If a career is a journey, then each job is a step along the way. Every job you take on will either progress your career or will hold it back. Sometimes we have little choice but to tread water in our career, taking any job that is available in order to survive. If you want to double your salary, you have to minimize time spent in jobs that are not giving you skills and experience to further your career.

I feel it is helpful to have even a rough idea of what job you might end up in that would show you have arrived in terms of your career: an ideal job. Your ideal job may not ultimately be the final one you have. You may gain your ideal job only to find it isn't suited to you. However, you will hopefully have gained skills and experiences along the way that will allow you to change direction without losing all of the benefits you've gained. There's no reason why you can't have more than one career in a lifetime and many jobs throughout a career.

I've found online job sites to be the most useful as I've tried to work out what my ideal job might be. Most sites allow you to apply a variety of filters to job searches that narrow the number of results being returned. If you are serious about doubling your salary, then you probably want to start by setting a filter on salary that is at least double your current salary.

If you've already applied some filters for job type and location, it's quite possible that you'll get no results being returned. A sign that you've overly restricted the filters. Remove all filters apart from salary and try again. Then you may find that you see jobs being returned that bear no relationship to the type of job you are searching for. That's often because you've entered a type of job that acts as a keyword for many different job types. For example, on one job site I tried searching for jobs matching "Joiner" (thinking carpentry) and received results including:

- Accountant
- Estate Agent
- Litigation Associate
- Finance Manager
- Recruitment Manager

In the job descriptions of several of these I found phrases similar to "a new joiner" and in one of them Joiner was the surname of the recruitment manager!

I did another search for "Baker" and received the following results:

- Head of Estates & Master Planning
- Senior Proposals Manager
- Solution Architect
- Lead .NET Developer

When I checked the detail of the job descriptions, it turned out the search was picking up "Baker" as a company name!

I tried changing "Joiner" to "Carpenter" and found one contract role being advertised with equivalent annual salary of £80,000. There were also two "Construction Manager" contract roles possibly paying between £275 and £500 per day. I suspect if joinery or carpentry is your skill set, then there are likely to be many more potential jobs that never see the online job sites. It's quite likely it's a case of who you know…

I dropped the salary level of "Baker" and started to see some results. Perhaps my initial salary goal was too high, or maybe there are jobs out there paying more, but which are advertised infrequently. I've seen this when searching for

"Systems Analyst". While there are junior level roles occasionally advertised, it is less common to see adverts for a more senior and better paid role. Just because you search once and don't find what you're looking for doesn't mean jobs won't be advertised later on. Be willing to keep searching over time.

A few years ago, I was researching more senior roles trying to get a handle on what skills I should be developing. Here's an analysis of one role that quite appealed to me:

"Senior BI ETL Architect: £60,000 - £75,000 per annum + bonus & benefits"

BI stands for Business Intelligence and implies the role involves working with databases and automating business reports.

ETL stands for Extract Transform Load and means the job will involve developing automated process for extracting data from databases, modifying the data, and loading data into the other databases.

As you can imagine, including the terms senior and architect implies they want someone with experience, someone who has possibly managed others, certainly someone who has managed projects, and someone who can not only do the job, but can draw up design plans to enable other people to do the job.

The job description contained a few useful sections.

"You will ideally be familiar with all aspects of the entire Data Warehousing project lifecycle from strategy development and requirements gathering through to solution design and implementation and will need to demonstrate this with a strong CV detailing previous client engagements and work history."

This paragraph confirmed and put some meat on the bones of the job title. A data warehouse is a database designed to hold summarized data to be used in reports. The job would involve ensuring the design was flexible enough to allow users to obtain the information they needed, while also condensing the data so reports would run quickly. They wanted someone who could manage the project from beginning to end, who was comfortable interviewing clients and working with people who might not always know initially what they want.

"The successful candidate would be typically involved in one or more projects in a variety of key technical roles within a typical Data Warehousing project lifecycle such as
Pre-sales support, Solution Architect
EDW Lead, Test Lead
Developer, Tester etc."

"involved in one or more projects" and "Pre-sales support" implied the role was working for a software company or consultancy. The list of technical roles includes "EDW Lead" which tells us they are looking for someone with experience of working on Enterprise level Data Warehouses. They are also looking for someone comfortable working in all essential roles including developer and tester.

"Significant experience (3-4yrs plus) in elements of the following:
Business Objects
Data Integrator
Microsoft SQL Server
Integration Services
Analysis Services"

This list of software experience was the icing on the cake. It clearly laid out the types of software I would need to gain experience of if I aspired to this sort of role and the amount of experience I would need. Business Objects and Analysis Services are used to develop reports. Data Integrator and Integration Services are two similar software packages used to develop ETL (Extract Transform Load) processes. Microsoft SQL Server is a database environment.

In reality I would expect someone to require at least ten years' experience of the software and different types of roles before they would be qualified for this level of role, but this one job advert acts as a sort of road map. If someone can gain the experience listed and prove themselves competent, they stand a good chance of securing an interview and being considered for the role. With the right level of experience and skill that person could expect to receive a salary between Sixty and Seventy-Five thousand pounds. Plus bonus… and benefits…

Not quite as much as a skilled footballer can command but not to be sniffed at either…

Why not try a similar analysis of your own ideal job looking to see if this can help you identify the skills and experience you need to develop?

The roles I've been looking at above are clearly sitting at the top of the pyramid and there are not that many roles like these out there. Does that mean it is harder to achieve these types of roles? Yes, absolutely!

You may need to work in several stepping-stone roles on the way to achieving your ideal job. In each one you can gain valuable experience and skills.

I've focused a lot on IT and contracting in this book because that's where I've had the most success and most recent experience. But going right back to my first couple of roles, I doubled my salary first of all by choosing to get training, by working hard, and by being in the right place at the right time.

I believe we make our own luck. I've seen a lot of colleagues just getting by, counting the minutes until home time, not caring about the company or the customers. I'm ashamed to admit that at times in my working life I've been no better. It takes a lot of discipline to go to work determined to work hard every single day. Even more when extra effort goes unrewarded.

If you are on a low salary right now, is it because you don't work hard? Is it because you have never tried applying for better paid jobs? Is it because you've never asked your boss what you would need to do to get a salary increase? Have you acquired training or extra education in the type of work you are doing?

It is important to look and find out what the top people in your chosen field earn. Do they earn that because of their knowledge or experience or artistry or a combination of all three? This will give you an idea of how much work you may need to put in and how much time it will take for you to reach your salary goal.

Unless you start asking yourself questions, researching and even asking others, you'll never discover what other possibilities exist.

Some benefits of education

For all my issues with education, I've never been able to completely turn my back on it. After leaving school I took two additional O Grade (Nat 5 equivalent) level exams between 1988 and 1995: Physics and Biology. The Youth Training Scheme included college modules and I gained a few more Scotvec certificates. I took a distance learning course through London Bible College and even signed up to The Writers Bureau back in the nineties. I've always read widely, consuming newspaper articles, wading through technical and scientific journals when I become interested in a topic.

Looking back, I'm convinced that education has been crucial in enabling me to double my salary. If I had not signed up for the Youth Training Scheme (YTS) in the late eighties, I would not have gone on to double my salary that first time. Every couple of months I'd get a visit from my trainer who would interview me to find out what I was doing and what competencies I'd developed. The YTS often seemed like it was about making sure I kept ticking boxes so that I could get a certificate, yet that had a side effect that for me at least was unexpected. Becoming aware of what the trainer was looking for meant I started to examine my actions. I was learning to analyse my own work and that is an extremely valuable skill to have.

If you as an employee can examine your work and find ways of doing things better, then your manager doesn't have to worry about you. If you extend this practice, you can develop yourself to a point where you can not only show you have new skills, but also show how you have improved. Going into any job interview and being able to talk through that shows a high degree of competence.

If I hadn't gone to college in 2003, I doubt I would have been able to develop a career in IT. Because my tutors knew the standard of work I was capable of and my ethic in terms of attending and participating, they were happy to recommend me when a company contacted them looking for someone.

I found myself in a positive feedback loop. At college I not only sought to learn what I was being taught but tried to understand why I was being taught it and then find ways of using that knowledge. When I finally had an opportunity to use it, I was immediately able to apply the knowledge I'd gained. More than that, I almost acted like I still was at college, asking questions of my new employer, learning what my new employer wanted me to do, trying to understand why they wanted me to do it and finding out ways to produce the system they wanted.

That college course also allowed me to understand that I don't do well in situations where requirements are vague, where there is no end to the work, where expectations are unreasonable. It did this by making it clear how we would be marked and graded, by giving us clear instructions and guidelines for our assignments, and by giving fixed deadlines. I've found myself comparing every job I've had since to that college course. Jobs where the work has been more project based are ones where I've done well. Jobs that consist of what I call business as usual (BAU) have usually led to me being frustrated unless I was able to convert the work into more of a project form.

Carrying on to complete a university degree has allowed me to develop additional skills that I still use today. The Java courses through the OU undoubtedly gave me an edge walking into the Sun interview but they also gave me confidence that I knew a particular methodology for programming. This, combined with the fact I now had experience in three different programming languages (Visual Basic for Microsoft Office, Jade, and Java), gave me confidence I could learn a fourth!

By the time I went for my interview at HarperCollins, I was close to completing my university degree. I had been exposed to ways of dealing with large complex projects through the OU course on systems thinking and was able to refer to that in the interview.

Professionals in all fields will make an effort to continue educating themselves throughout their careers. They will always see learning as an important part of their lives. What that education will look like, how it will work in practice will differ from profession to profession and individual to individual, but it will continue. If you want to double your salary, you should determine to act like a professional, to seek to constantly increase your knowledge, to develop new skills and expand your experience.

How do you pay for education when you have no money?

When your income is low, how do you fund training and education to enable you to earn more? It can seem like one of those catch-22 situations. Back in 2003, I wasn't able to afford the course fees for college.

Ray Bradbury, the author of Fahrenheit 451, famously said: "I spent three days a week for 10 years educating myself in the public library, and it's better than college. People should educate themselves—you can get a complete education for no money."

There is a lot of truth to this, but unfortunately employers prefer to see subjects studied through approved training providers or at school, college and university rather than at a library when reviewing your CV.

If, like me, you left school with average qualifications (or even none at all) you will always be struggling to compete with others who have a college certificate or degree. This is in spite of the contrary reality that experience usually trumps education. But how do you get that experience if an employer won't employ you?

This was my experience for years. I applied for jobs that I knew I could do but was rejected, often even before the interview stage. When employers—who are usually pushed for time—get dozens of applications for one job, they have to whittle down those applications to a manageable number. If your CV is competing with dozens who have the same experience as you but who also have a better education, yours will be the CV that is dropped!

In 2003, many of the job adverts I was looking at stated they wanted someone with a degree. But studying three years full time to get a degree meant I would not be able to provide for my family. Despite having had a long love/hate relationship with formal education, I realised I needed to get over that as it was likely to enable me to get a better paid job.

A memory of a colleague who had been studying for a Higher National Certificate in Computing kept coming back to me. You could study for an HNC through night classes over two years while continuing to work. It would be tough but far better than being completely broke for three years and probably going into debt.

Having decided on trying for a career in computing/IT, I applied to join the HNC Computing course. I can't remember now how I found out that I might be eligible for a bursary grant—for people on low income— towards tuition fees but I was, and that grant covered the whole cost of the first year's tuition! If your income is low, it is always worth asking if a similar scheme exists when applying to college or university. You can even ask for help completing the forms!

By the second year I had started my first IT contract and, with my wife also working, our income had risen to the point where I had to pay the course fees. Rising income is a good problem to have!

My Open University course M256 Software Development with Java was mostly paid for by Tesco Clubcard tokens. For a few short years, the retailer Tesco agreed with the Open University to issue vouchers towards OU courses in exchange for their shopping vouchers. But not only that, they gave OU vouchers to four times the value! The £380 fee for the course was reduced to only £90 after we had used those vouchers!

We were able to agree to pay the other OU courses through instalments at between £60 and £100 a month at a fairly low rate of interest. There was never a time when we felt we had enough saved up to pay the whole course fee in one lump sum. Spreading the cost at a low interest rate was for us the best option at that time.

If we had paid the full cost of my higher education, it would have looked like this:

	Cost of Course
HNC Year 1	£400.00
HNC Year 2	£400.00
M255	£380.00
M256	£380.00
T306	£649.89
T306 (additional materials)	£60.75
A215	£662.29
	£2,932.93

In reality we only paid £2,242,93:

	Paid for Course
HNC Year 1	£0.00
HNC Year 2	£400.00
M255	£380.00
M256	£90.00
T306	£649.89
T306 (additional materials)	£60.75
A215	£662.29
	£2,242.93

Maybe that still looks like a lot of money, but remember, this was spread out over many years and the reduction in course fees made a huge difference at the time.

I graduated from university with no debt, though it took me eight years and a lot of lost evenings and weekends. Compare that with what young adults in England today are facing as they are enticed onto full time university courses:

	Annual cost	Total cost after three years
Tuition	£9,250	£27,750
Living costs	£7,500	£22,500
		£50,250

In Scotland it is easier with the Scottish government paying the tuition fees, yet many courses in Scotland are four years long leading some young adults to rack up debt of £30,000. It makes no sense to me that government continues to encourage children to go to university full time when many will choose to take degrees that offer no entry to a career that would allow them to pay off that debt and start really earning and saving. It seems like we are encouraging our children to become a type of indentured slaves, forever owing the government a debt they will never be able to pay off.

I don't believe there is any point in going to university and building up debts to study a subject when you have no idea what you want to do with your life. If someone is offering you a free education along with a grant towards food and accommodation, then by all means grab that offer. But if you are going to leave university after three years, tens of thousands of pounds in debt and with a qualification that is no use to you, I don't care how much your eyes have been opened to the world around you, or that you've been taught to learn, you were sold a pig in a poke.

While I'm thinking about education, I've never understood why teenagers get free or reduced fees for education, but adults are expected to pay full price. My experience as a teenager was of having no idea what I wanted to do with my life. Why is it that teenagers who are more likely to make the wrong choice about their education are given such a wonderful gift when adults, who are far better placed to decide, have to pay?

I get that government sees sending teenagers to university as a better option than them being unemployed, yet it would make far more sense to create actual jobs and give teenagers experience of working while using their energy and talents to do something useful for society.

I do think that higher education can be of real use to you in many different career paths; however part time study is a far safer option than full time unless you can afford to take that time off. Working while I studied, I was able to benefit both my employer and my grades as I applied what I learned in both situations to each other.

Will education enable you to double your salary?

Education worked for me because I knew there were jobs in the career I had chosen that paid double what I was able to earn at the time. Education worked because it was directly related to my chosen career. Education worked because I chose to devote myself to learning and apply what I was learning in my career. Education worked because I took responsibility for my learning, understanding early on that it wasn't my tutors' or lecturers' responsibility to teach me but my responsibility to learn, to ask questions, to challenge.

I must make clear that I went to college and later took university courses precisely because I didn't know what I needed to know. And for me those courses taught me a lot of what I needed to know. Education then opened doors to jobs where I was able to learn more. I'm sure there are still many things that would be useful to know and maybe I will return to higher education in the future, or maybe I'll continue to learn through the workplace or personal study.

If, like I did, you do need an education, spend time working out what course(s) to take. Adults returning to higher education after gaining years of life experience are far more likely to know what they need or what they want. That motivation is why mature students tend to get better grades in their chosen subjects.

Knowing what you need or want to study will help you set a goal to achieve your chosen qualification. Having set that goal, you can then turn your mind to how to pay for it!

If you have savings or earn enough that this isn't an issue for you, fantastic! If not, or even if you are utterly broke, there is no reason why you cannot set an additional goal to raise the funding you will need. Focusing on the goals of achieving a qualification and raising funding for that qualification opens your mind to possibilities. Your brain begins to work out ways of solving any problems – this can happen without you even realising. The number of times I've had a problem and it's only when I've put some distance between myself and the situation that the solution appears!

I've read several respected life coaching experts say the same thing. Our subconscious mind is capable of directing us to solutions if we'll simply give ourselves a chance. Sometimes that solution can take weeks or months to take form. Sometimes we find we need to make radical changes before we can find a solution.

If you have some money and are in work, then consider studying through distance learning or night classes to allow you to learn while still earning.

If you have no money at all, you may be eligible for a grant or bursary to offset some or all of the course fees. It costs nothing to ask!

Keep an open mind. Higher education courses may only be necessary if you are seeking certain careers as an employee. They can be useful to the self-employed entrepreneur, but you may find there are now a wealth of freely available courses that can impart a similar level of knowledge. You are not going to receive one-on-one mentoring from a YouTube series, but can learn a lot from watching and listening to the millions of short movies that are uploaded there.

Remember that Ray Bradbury quote at the start of this chapter about libraries? What would he have made of the Internet?

YouTube is only one website among many that offers free to watch content you can use to improve your knowledge and skills. My son introduced me to codecademy.com which offers free training in several software languages. Several people have encouraged me to use the Duolingo app to learn another language. Whatever your skill-set, it is likely there is a website or app out there you can use.

Finally, there may also be the option of getting paid to train. You may find an apprenticeship is open to you, one that pays more than an allowance, allowing you to earn a basic wage while learning valuable skills. A junior role in a company can be just as good, if you are willing to learn all you can and take on whatever challenges are thrown at you.

Investigate all options, keep looking, ask questions, you might be surprised at what is available.

Interview techniques

I used to dread interviews, now I almost look forward to them. What changed?

My first interview consisted of my father asking a local shopkeeper if he had a job I could do. I was looked up and down as we stood in the shop and asked a couple of simple questions. I'm not sure if I got the job because of my father's reputation or because the shopkeeper desperately needed someone, though maybe a bit of both. I don't think I was an especially good candidate or interviewee; however I started the next week.

Despite having worked for my father on Saturdays and in school holidays while growing up, working a full five day week proved to be tiring. It toughened me up and gradually I learned to pace myself, learned where the stock was on all the shelves, so I could quickly answer customers' queries. I also sought to gain additional knowledge about what customers were looking for and why.

My next interview was for the Youth Training Scheme position and I confess I don't remember much about that experience. But I was accepted.

Three years later I interviewed for a part time supervisor's role at the other end of the country. The boy from the Northern Isles bounced into that interview, pony tail flying behind me. I was twenty-one, newly married, full of confidence with a smart answer for every question.

I suspect the two women interviewing me thought I would be a breath of fresh air. Within two weeks I'd managed to turn my team against me and spent the next two years actually learning how to manage others. My confidence knocked down, it was years before I could confidently walk into an interview.

Without any career plans I drifted from job to job. I must have picked up some interview skills, but often found the jobs I really wanted were the ones I couldn't even get an interview for, then on the odd occasion I did, I performed abysmally. Desperation is not a good quality to display during an interview.

I only really began to enjoy interviews after I interviewed for Barclays back in 2007. For the first time I was sent a pack to help me prepare for the interview. They were going to use the S.T.A.R. scoring system as part of a competency-based interview.

- Situation
- Task
- Action
- Result

I spent several evenings preparing for that interview. I couldn't see a long-term future at the company I worked for and was seriously looking to leave, but being in a permanent role meant I didn't have to show it.

Also, for the first time in my life, I'd been head hunted. I was able to walk into that interview able to say that an agency had contacted me and that I was interested in the opportunity. Believe me, that sounds a lot better than I hate my job and would do anything to get out!

Competency based interviews take a lot of preparation if you've never done one before, but it is time well spent. While at Barclays I had the opportunity to be an interviewer during a large recruitment drive. Interviewers will never have enough hours in the day. They desperately want to find the right person to fill a role, so they can stop interviewing and get back to their job. If you can structure your answers to help them see you are the right person, they will be delighted.

In well managed competency interviews there are a set of questions which every candidate will get asked. The pack, which contained dozens of sample questions, explained that I was expected to explain a situation relevant to the question, What task I was asked to perform, what action I took, and what the result was.

Candidates are then scored on a simple 1 to 5 by each interviewer on each question. The answers are then totalled and where two interviewers are involved, an average is given. This ensures everyone is given a fair chance to do well.

In addition to preparing for the competency interview I did a lot of research on Barclays, taking notes in case I needed to refer to them in my interview. Those notes included things like:

- What the company did
- The current share price
- The last year's profit and revenue for the group and the division.
- Where the company operated
- Number of employees
- Things I found interesting about the company
- Questions I wanted to ask.

I walked into the competency interview more confident than I ever had. Nervous of course, but with the knowledge I'd done everything I could to prepare.

The interview went well. There were one or two times when I had to think through an answer and I may have asked to have another go at a question, but none of this was counted against me. Good interviewers know that people are nervous and that being under pressure means that more time will be required to think through an answer.

In addition to the more standard interview I also had a technical interview with other team members and then a practical test. The technical interview also went well. I was well experienced by that point in the software I would be using. It was good to finally be asked questions that I could easily answer.

The practical test was a clever addition. I'd previously had psychometric testing which may have given some insight into my problem-solving abilities but told the company nothing about how I actually worked.

Given a set of data I had to follow a series of instructions to create a report. I took off my jacket, sat down at the laptop and got on with it. Half an hour later I'd completed the list of instructions and was thinking I'd want to give candidates a similar challenge if I was ever the interviewer for a technical role.

I was offered the role, I accepted, and have used the experience as I've prepared for every interview since. This hasn't meant that I've been accepted for every job I've interviewed for since then, but I've continued to feel far happier about interviewing.

Not that everything has gone as I'd have hoped...

I interviewed for one role and was then asked to come back for a second interview with a more senior manager at 6PM a day or two later. I turned up at quarter to six and found the building locked down. I was let into an empty reception by an employee who was leaving so phoned up to the manager who was to interview me, to let him know I was in reception. I got voicemail so left a message.

I didn't receive a response and by five to six decided to call again knowing that it's easy to miss voicemail messages. Again, straight to voicemail.

More people came through reception, leaving for the night.

At 6PM I called again. Left more voicemail. No-one was visible. I was beginning to wonder how I'd exit the building if I wasn't able to get in touch with the manager...

A few minutes after 6PM the manager came down and his first statement was: "You didn't need to keep calling, I knew you were here."

My heart sank. I thought I'd done well in the first interview, but right from the start had managed to irritate this interviewer. Plus, if this guy didn't realise there was no way for me to know that he knew, what was the rest of the interview going to be like? I took a deep breath and put on my professional poker face. I was there, I might as well give the interview all I had.

I think the interview went okay from that point. At the end of the interview he asked me how I dealt with change. This is one of those tricky interview questions that can trick you up. Some interviewers seem to delight in using them while others avoid them.

I don't know why I answered the way I did. I told him that at age thirty I realised I had a wife, two children and no career. I decided to change my life. I went to college and took night classes for two years. I took every job I could get, studied in my own time and built up a set of skills that I could use. I told him that for the last few years I had done all I could to transform my life and had embraced change.

I finished my speech a little out of breath and sat looking at him, wondering if I'd overdone it. He nodded and said it was a good answer. I was offered the job.

Interviews can take a left turn but being willing to roll with it and remain professional can set you apart from other candidates.

However, some left turns are clear signs it's time to walk out of the door. A friend shared that he was once asked what kind of underwear he was wearing. "Boxers," he replied without missing a beat. "Good," the interviewer said. "If you'd said briefs, I'd have struck you off."

I've not yet walked out of an interview but if I had been asked something that strange, I might well have.

I have experienced interviewers trying to trip me up and others who have been unprepared or incompetent. With more confidence now, I see these situations as being valuable to the interviewee, revealing a lot about the interviewer and potentially about the company. It can be awkward and embarrassing to be asked questions that seem designed to humiliate, but if you're in a job, the benefit is you get an insight into their company before you hand in your notice to your current employer. And if you don't have a job then you can decide whether the pain of working for such an individual is something you can put up with while continuing to look for the right job.

While competency interviews are becoming more and more common, even if a company doesn't use that method, you as the interviewee can still take advantage of it. At its most basic, a competency interview expects you to answer each question in three parts:

- What the situation was
- How you responded
- What the results were

If you practise structuring your answers in this way, you can develop an ability to respond clearly to interview questions. It will also be helpful if you can fill out your answer by stating why the situation was important and who was affected or benefitted from your actions. This allows you to give a complete answer.

It's not always clear what the interviewer is asking. Don't be afraid to ask: would you mind rephrasing the question? It might be the question was actually clear and any other time you would have been able to answer it, but stress in interviews can play on our mind and it is, or should be, acceptable to ask for clarification. A company that penalises you for seeking clarification is one to be avoided.

If you get a sense that the interviewer is struggling themselves, try and make their job easier. Some helpful questions might be:

"Would it help if I described a situation where I was asked to do this task?"

"I noticed in the advert for the role that you were looking for someone with experience of... May I tell you about my experience in this area?"

Not every manager has the opportunity to receive training in how best to carry out interviews. Volunteering relevant information about your skills and experience can assist them in making a decision.

A question may seem to steer you away from the best answer you could give and so sometimes I find it is best to be willing to use the politician's method of choosing to answer the question I think should have been asked. If you do this, always be willing to return to the question if the interviewer isn't convinced by your answer, using the most appropriate situation to the question. If you do this, it may also be advisable to caveat your initial answer with an acknowledgment that you're not sure if this is the most relevant answer you could give...

When applying for a role that pays more than your current or previous role, it's always a concern you might be asked what your previous salary or day rate was. If there is only a ten percent difference, it won't make any difference. Even twenty percent might not matter. But the higher the difference, the more awkward I feel.

The last thing I want in an interview is for the interviewer to start thinking I can't be suitable for the job because I've not been able to earn whatever the interviewer thinks is the minimum threshold.

None of us want to lie and I would always advise choosing honesty over deceit. However, this is an unfair question. It should make no difference what we previously were earning if we are capable of and are willing to take on a job.

One fortunate side benefit of contracting is that I can now explain that contracts with previous employers prevent me discussing the day rate received.

If this is a concern for you when applying for a contract role, simply state what your day rate is: "My day rate is £250 a day." You haven't lied about your previous rate, simply sidestepped the question.

If you are applying for a role where the salary offered is substantially above what you are currently earning, you need to be sure you can justify that increase. If you can't you are wasting both your and their time. Gather your evidence, prepare a solid case, consider arguments against you earning that much and practise reasoned responses to those arguments. If you can present good evidence and politely and reasonably demonstrate why you are worth earning a higher salary, you may well be given the opportunity to continue to prove it while being paid for the privilege.

Always remember that you are not the only person being interviewed. By this I don't mean you are going up against other candidates for the role, I mean you are also interviewing the employer! We spend a third of our adult lives at work and we should make every effort to decide whether the time we give to an employer is time we are happy to give. You need to be careful with this attitude because there are probably less employers comfortable with this reality than we would wish. Asking what a typical day in the role would entail, asking what challenges you will face, what your short- and long-term priorities will be in the role; all these sorts of questions can give you valuable insight into the company. Interview technique is a skill that can be learned. I know because I've managed to do so. You can too!

The best suit you'll ever wear

If you've never worn a suit to work, I can almost guarantee that if you do wear one, you'll have someone ask if you're going to a job interview!

We're programmed to notice change, though why I'm oblivious to my wife's new haircut and instantly notice when someone makes an effort to dress smartly at work I can't say!

Forgive me if this chapter seems mostly irrelevant to women. Women seem to have a far greater range of options when it comes to smart business clothes. Yet I'm also aware that wide range of options is far more limiting than it appears. I don't consider myself in any way knowledgeable about what women wear but am more than happy to hear your views.

It's not essential that you wear a suit to work if you want to progress your career and double your salary, but how you dress is vitally important. What we wear influences our thinking, it influences the people around us. It tells other people a lot about who we think we are.

If you are a plumber, turning up to a client's house in a suit will most likely give the wrong impression. Turning up in a clean and pressed uniform however might just set you apart from the guy who quoted for the job yesterday, whose jeans were torn and his t-shirt should have been washed three weeks ago.

People are constantly evaluating other people. We might have been told not to judge a book by its cover, but we cannot help judging people by their hair style, their body odour, the type and state of the clothes they wear, and of course—their shoes.

In whatever field of work you want to earn money, how you dress and present yourself will have an impact on the likelihood of whether other people will want to pay you, and how much they will be willing to pay you.

I think I was four when I was given my first suit. A bright purple pinstripe that possibly was in vogue in the seventies. I can't recall if I'd had a say in choosing it or was forced to wear it, only that I distinctly remember, as soon as I got the opportunity, rolling around on the grass.

There wasn't much call to wear a suit in the shop where I started working, or in the store. At some point I must have bought a suit myself, a shiny light, grey suit that I wore on special occasions. Strangely enough, it was while I was in Tajikistan that I started wearing a suit to work daily. It was part of the culture there that professional men wore suits to work and I knew it made sense to fit in.

Returning to the UK I didn't have much call to wear suits, working from home for the travel company. Even on my first IT contract and the next few roles I had, I think I only wore a suit for the job interviews.

Flush with money from that first IT contract, I'd actually gone out and bought two suits, a smart grey one and a regular black funeral suit. Everyone needs a black suit, right? Both were off the rack, but the grey one properly fitted me. I can remember putting it on in the shop and it just felt right. When I looked in the mirror, it was as if the suit had been made for me.

I've always dressed smart for job interviews, but I felt good walking into interviews dressed in that suit. Like I belonged there. Interviews had always been incredibly scary experiences, but a combination of events took away most of my fear and, even if I don't always look forward to them now, I now see them as a normal part of life. Finding a suit that suited me helped a lot with that.

For several years I chose to put on smart trousers and a shirt when heading out to work, leaving my suit in the wardrobe, the suit that made me feel good when I wore it. Then, I think while working at Sun Microsystems, I realised that if wearing the suit made me feel good about myself, maybe I should wear it all the time. And so I did. And I did start to feel better about myself.

Eventually that suit wore out and I needed a replacement. A couple of years ago I went to a local store and again bought a suit off a rack. A three piece suit this time. I'd never worn one, had even looked down on the idea of wearing a waistcoat, but now I doubt I'll ever go back! The beauty of the waistcoat is that it hides your crumpled shirt, something that I could never seem to prevent. Throughout the day I would always have to be tucking my shirt back in. Now, the waistcoat hides that.

I wear a suit almost every day, sometimes even on dress down Fridays. I'm projecting an image of professionalism, which helps focus my thoughts and even allows me to avoid interactions that destroy professionalism.

One final thought on suits: brown, white, black or blue, what colour should you wear? Ronald Reagan was president of the USA for eight of my childhood years. One comment about him that has always stuck with me is that he was one of the few people who could get away with wearing a brown suit. Really? I suspect quite a few people look better in brown suits than in other colours.

Tom Hanks stood out like a sore thumb when he turned up at the office party wearing a white tuxedo in the movie Big. Yet that naive act helped bring him to the attention of the company boss and also win the girl. Okay, it was just a movie, but our clothing choices do have an impact.

A light blue suit became a plot device for Alexander's brother in the movie Alexander and the Terrible, Horrible, No Good, Very Bad Day. While the suit never really worked for the brother, it did contribute to him realising how shallow his girlfriend was and allowing him to decide she wasn't someone he wanted to be with.

Will Smith was told the black suit was the last he would ever wear in another movie: Men In Black. Maybe he did make that suit look cool, but you don't have to limit yourself to one colour of suit.

That's a lot of movie references... Dress appropriately for your work and make an effort for every interview you attend. Find clothes that are comfortable to wear and that make you feel good about yourself, while also being smart. You'll be glad you did.

A better CV

I detest job application forms. Some are worse than others, but almost all of them seem to be a frustrating waste of time. If the objective is to determine who can read and follow instructions then maybe there is a purpose, but a long time ago I decided I wanted to do more with my career than simply read and follow instructions.

Yet if you want to apply for a different and hopefully better paying job you will likely have to make sure you fill in paper or online forms as required otherwise your application won't even be read. Unless they accept a CV instead...

If you want to progress in your career, you have to have a CV. I'd hope you know what a CV is if you're reading this book, but why should I assume that? A Curriculum Vitae is a list and description of your work and relevant experience. Usually only one or two pages long, it should concisely tell a prospective employer all they need to know to allow them to decide whether or not to offer to interview you.

There are many different templates you can use for your CV and while some are considered current and recommended, the important thing to know is you have some flexibility with the format you use.

You absolutely should include your contact details at the top on the first page and at a bare minimum:

- Name
- Location
- Mobile phone number
- Email address

If you have set up a LinkedIn profile including your experience, I would also recommend adding the LinkedIn URL to your CV contact details.

If you don't have a mobile phone, then you must get one if you are applying for jobs. A cheap pay-as-you-go phone is fine just so long as you carry it with you and it's always on so agencies or employers can contact you. You can no longer expect anyone to leave a message on a landline answering service/machine. If you are unavailable, there are likely dozens if not hundreds of other candidates who are more than likely ready to answer a call.

You must also have an email address. This should be professional with preferably your first and last name before the @ symbol and a non-offensive domain afterwards. I would advise avoiding Hotmail and Yahoo free email accounts. I know too many people who find incoming emails to those services end up in spam folders. If you can afford it and are willing to set it up, it does not cost a lot to buy your own web site domain name and a cheap hosting service that would allow you to use your very own email account. For less than £40 a year, in some cases much less, you could have an email address like <firstname> . <lastname> @ <someprofessionalsoundingdomain.co.uk>

Some CV guidance suggests including a personal statement next. I don't on my CV, but if you are able to craft a compelling summary of who you are and why you should be hired, some employers will look for this.

A number of years ago I was advised to include a short summary of key skills and this now sits below my contact details:

Principal skills	Level of experience
SQL and Database development (SQL Server 2000-2012, Oracle 8-10g, MS Access 2000-2016), DTS, SSIS, ETL	10 years
VBA Programming and MI development in Microsoft Access, Excel, Word (2000-2016), Visual Basic Programming in StarOffice Calc	10 years
Business Analysis, Full Lifecycle Systems Analysis, Design and Testing	7 years
Business Objects XI Universe, Webi, dashboard, data warehouse and scheduling development; SSRS; Oracle Business Intelligence (OBIEE)	5 years
Project and Team Management, Mentoring and Training	4 years

At a glance, recruiters can see how much experience I have in the key skills and software I've used. Even better, as most agencies now request CVs are emailed to them, they can store the CV in their database and if they are searching for any skills that appear on my CV, I will be more likely to be contacted.

It used to be people were advised to list education before work experience and if you have just left school or university without any or much work experience, this may well look better. If you have work experience though, no matter how little, I would list that next. Relevant work experience trumps education in most circumstances.

Include the name of the company or organization you work or worked for. If you were employed by an agency, with the agency paying you instead of the employer, then also include the name of the agency. Include the date you started work and finished work. Unless you are still working there in which case state "To present".

Include the address of the company you worked for, and the job title you were given. Then include a brief description of the work you did. It's important to be positive here. If you developed or created something, mention that, and also if you achieved anything out of the ordinary. Be specific. State "I processed an average of 500 orders a day" rather than "I was responsible for processing orders".

I confess that my descriptions are far from brief and my current CV runs to five pages rather than the maximum recommended two pages. Because most employers and agencies are looking for at least three to five years' experience and due to the nature of my work as a contractor, I work for an average of three employers every year. Also, I rarely do the same type of contract in a row. All employers and agencies are most interested in your most recent work experience. Since I've a fairly broad range of skills and experience I include more examples of my work experience than most people will need.

I have taken to including just a one-line summary of older contracts, but as I also provide a link to my LinkedIn profile where all of my relevant experience can still be viewed with detailed descriptions, employers can review this if they wish.

If you are struggling to fit all your experience on one or two pages, don't panic. I also include a statement: "Full employment history available on request" after the list of experience. This lets recruiters know they can obtain your full work history if required.

Your education and all training courses, completed or in progress, should come next. The most relevant courses should be shown first, unless none of your courses are directly relevant, in which case the highest level courses and/or certificates should be shown first. I no longer include school certificates on my CV. Some employers still demand them on job applications which seems redundant. If you have obtained a higher education certificate, this should demonstrate a greater level of ability than school certificates and negate the need to provide details of these. However, I acknowledge that I scraped a pass on some of my school exams which feeds my reluctance to include those results. If you achieved high grades, then you may want to include that detail. If like me you only achieved average results and have no higher level certificates, remember that a pass is still a pass and for the first fifteen years I was working, that was all I had to include and so I did. Maybe if you are embarrassed about your school results you can use that to motivate you to continue with education or training…

If your work experience is less, then include all of your education achievements to fill out your CV.

It is not essential to include personal interests or hobbies. If you choose to do so, only include interests which have some relevance to the job in question, or those that will allow you to present a positive side of yourself in an interview.

Finally, you should include a statement: "References are available on request". Do not include references on your CV. You want to know if a recruiter wants to contact your references. Really a recruiter should not be contacting your references unless they have already offered you a job. Otherwise your referees' time may be wasted.

It is worth getting feedback on your CV from people you trust. Make sure you proofread it thoroughly and correct any spelling or grammar errors. If you don't have a computer or printer at home, your local library will have word processing software allowing you to create your CV, edit it, proof-read it and ultimately print it!

When your employer turns against you

It is important to remember that our employers are not our friends. Friendship can grow in an employer-employee relationship, but at the base level, the relationship should be purely professional. If we forget this, or allow the definition of our relationship to become blurred, if the relationship becomes too informal, it can have adverse consequences with respect and authority being diminished.

Unfortunately, there can be occasions where authority is abused—knowingly or unknowingly—and if we don't have a clear perspective on the relationship we can allow ourselves to remain a victim.

I expect two things from my employers:

- They will give me clear instructions
- They will pay me what I'm owed, on time and in full

If these two things happen then I expect like most people I can have a good relationship with my employer. If either does not happen, especially if there is repeated failure to give clear instructions or failure to pay me, I believe my employer has failed to meet their end of the contract.

Unclear instructions can include giving rushed and incomplete instructions, giving wrong instructions, or changing the instructions without acknowledging that the increase in workload may prevent the task being completed by the original deadline.

However, we have a responsibility to challenge unclear instructions, both to protect ourselves and our employer. If we know instructions are not clear and don't ask for clarification, do not insist on sufficient time being given to pass on the instructions, do not warn that there is insufficient time to complete the task, we share in the responsibility. It can be embarrassing to admit we don't understand what we've been asked to do, but in a professional relationship, there is responsibility on both sides. We can only interpret instructions based on our knowledge and experience.

"Just get it done!" might seem like a powerful, managerial statement. It's actually an aggressive, bullying and dismissive insult. If your employer speaks to you in this way, they are saying one or more of: you aren't important enough for me to waste my time explaining to you, I expect you to read my mind, your time and life doesn't matter, or you are my slave in all but name.

Of course, there are times when we are perfectly able to get things done, even tasks that may initially seem beyond us. It's not always a bad thing to be given a challenge that stretches us, forces us to learn, to research, to dream up new ways of doing things. But if your employer has respect for you, how they address you will be very different. It's one thing to be clearly told by your employer that they believe you are capable of taking on a difficult task and working out what needs to be done, quite another to be ordered around as if you had no rights.

I've had employers try and bully me in the past. I don't respond well to bullying. It won't make me work faster or harder and is likely to make me ask more questions than less, which I've noticed infuriates bullies. I've had attempts made to make me do things which I know or suspect to be illegal or unethical. My usual response is to ask for the instruction in writing which allows me to raise my concerns in response, in writing, thus forming an audit chain which at the least covers my back if I'm uncertain about the legal situation. Although I dislike being forced into a position where I feel I have no alternative, I have on some occasions refused an order. My reputation is too important to risk it.

That being said, this chapter is not about bullying, which is inexcusable in every circumstance. Instead I want to examine a few less serious situations I've found myself in, what it felt like for me and how I responded.

When the first part of the contract is broken

Mostly I don't mind management buzzwords. They can get a bit irritating at times, but some of them are so well known that they've become clichéd and so are actually useful. I recall one manager who liked his buzzwords. During one meeting where we were discussing how to prioritise tasks, he kept using one particular phrase: "Let's talk about this offline."

In my experience when you're online—on a conference call, Skype chat or Webex session—someone saying let's talk about this offline usually means they want to talk about it in private, after the meeting is over. We were in a face to face meeting and it sounded strange but hey, it meant the same thing, right?

Possibly not.

I was trying to set expectations for how long each task would take as I'd looked at the detail and needed my manager to be aware it was unlikely I could complete all of the tasks over the next week due to the extent of what was required. Each time I tried to talk about the detail in order to explain this, my manager cut me off, telling me we'd talk about it offline. He said we needed to remain focused and due to a lack of time could only discuss the most important tasks. I confess that I found myself utterly confused by this. As I understood it, we were meeting to set my priorities, so why would we put off discussing the issues that determined how long tasks would take? When I made it clear I would not be able to do all of the tasks again I was told: "Let's talk about this offline." I was forced to assume he wanted to talk about the detail later.

When we met again later that day, he pulled me up for not telling him why I wouldn't be able to do everything he wanted the following week. Taken aback, I felt I needed to explain the priorities I was planning to work to. He agreed that was reasonable but then reminded me that I needed to keep him informed of my planned workload.

It was quite clear he was rebuking me for not informing him of what I was planning to do. Then I remembered what he had kept telling me each time I tried to go into detail during the earlier meeting... "Let's talk about this offline."

I challenged him, reminded him that he told me he wanted to talk about this offline. He muttered something and quickly changed the subject.

I had gone into the original meeting expecting to discuss what I would be working on. Had been ready to explain the restrictions I was working on and had been prevented from explaining by my manager. Then I was rebuked for not giving him enough information. The first part of the unwritten contract was being broken.

I was being given contradictory signals from my manager and could see I was in a lose/lose situation. If I had ignored his orders to take it offline during the meeting, I would likely have been pulled up for it. His inability to recognise the contradictory signals he was giving meant a breakdown in trust between us. Worse than the loss of trust, his willingness to rebuke me for failing to do something after he denied me the chance to do it was a huge red flag that I would need to be careful around him. If he had apologised for making a mistake, then that would have been different; however I never received an apology.

Does that matter? Should employees expect their managers to acknowledge or apologize when they make mistakes? Of course. Even a simple "I got that wrong," or "I made a mistake," makes a big difference. The word sorry doesn't even have to be used, let alone the word apologize. Without the manager acknowledging responsibility though, the employee is left unable to trust their manager and that is the beginning of the end of the relationship.

At least for me. Some people do seem to enter into a twisted contract where they accept an effectively abusive relationship with a manager or organisation in exchange for believing they have the right to complain about whatever terrible thing that has happened.

I believe this is unhealthy. I believe it is unprofessional to complain about our managers and employer. If we feel a need to complain, it is far better to deal with the cause of the problem, as complaining to people who can't fix the problem does nothing to help anyone. I get that sometimes we need to unload and that by sharing our struggles, we can relieve tension. Yet if the actual cause of that tension and stress is not dealt with, there may be a long-term impact on our health and well-being.

I'm conscious that I could be accused of complaining through what I've written in this chapter. I'd welcome your comments and feedback on this. I've decided to share some of my negative experiences to give some balance. I don't always know what to do. Sometimes situations are bad and maybe we can do something to improve them, but sometimes we can't.

In the situation above, having defended myself to my manager, I didn't see anything else I could do. Knowing I was in a rolling short-term contract I quickly decided that if the situation became worse, I would either give notice that I wasn't planning to renew the contract or if my relationship deteriorated with my manager and I wasn't able to find a compromise in how we communicated, I would give notice early.

When the second part is broken

I had another case where mid contract I was asked to travel down to London. There had been no discussion of travel during the interview and my manager was blindsided by the request. My three children were still young and as my wife was working herself, going meant asking her to deal with the extra workload at home.

I think in some respects there is little difference between being a permanent employee and a contractor. Neither can afford to refuse too many times. The permanent employee who gets a reputation for being hard-headed can find themselves being side-lined and passed over when it comes to promotion and salary increase. The contractor may not have their contract renewed and in extreme cases can be simply asked to leave. I like to tell myself that in my current guise as a contractor I'm freer than a regular employee, but I know that isn't quite true.

I agreed to go, spent my own time preparing for the trip and inconvenienced myself by getting up at 4 am to allow me to fly down early and be in the London office for 9 am. (By the time the trip was over I had effectively lost three evenings that could have been spent with my family.)

It was a successful trip and was useful to meet the team members I'd only been talking with over the phone. That night, when I came to book myself into the hotel, things started to go wrong. I'd booked the hotel using my manager's credit card as I'd been instructed, yet the hotel wanted me to present the card, even though it had been pre-paid through the company online booking system. The booking system instructions had made it clear that all payments should be made on company credit cards, but to avoid sleeping on the street that night I had to pay on my own card. It was annoying but fair enough, I'd be reimbursed quickly, I thought.

I got home late the following evening and the next day I started putting together my expenses claim. £230 including the hotel, taxis and meals. I don't like the thought that I, as a contractor, am subsidising a large organisation—even for a few days. There is just something wrong that an employee or contractor should be expected to give an interest free loan to their employer, but unable to see a way round it, I sucked it up.

My manager had to approve my use of the expenses claim system before I could submit my claim. He took a fair while to do this. Fair enough. He is busy, and I can't expect my manger to jump when I tell him, right?

Then, having approved my use of the expenses claim system he had to approve the actual expenses. This had to be done before 5 pm on a Monday to be paid that Friday. He failed to approve them. Not only that, he also failed to approve my timesheet that week.

It wasn't the first time he'd failed to approve my timesheet on time and now this was starting to seem like the second part of the unwritten contract was being broken.

He didn't sign my timesheet or approve my expenses the next day either. Not that it would have made much practical difference as I could not be paid for another week anyway, but it would have made a difference. An apology would have made a difference. It would have shown that I was valuable, that I as an employee deserved to get paid and while mistakes happen and sometimes there are delays, the intention was there to keep the unwritten contract.

I use the term unwritten contract deliberately since I've never had a contract where there are penalties for the employer if they fail to pay the employee on time. Why not? As a contractor this would make a lot of sense. I take on a huge amount of risk as a contractor and yet in most contracts I end up signing, there is a clause that says I am responsible for my manager approving my timesheet, with no clause stating what the penalties are if a manager fails to approve the timesheet in a reasonable time…

Does that make legal sense? Does it make moral or ethical sense? I don't think so. I absolutely have a responsibility to present my timesheet early enough in the day that my manager has time to sign it, remembering that nowadays many timesheets are electronic and online. So why don't managers have responsibility to sign timesheets before the cut-off?

In this case, my manager said he had lost his password for the approval system.

Fair enough. Well, I didn't think that at the time but perhaps I should have given him the benefit of the doubt. Then again, maybe not as he didn't sign it the following day, or the next. However, he did find time to give me clear instructions. The first part of the unwritten contract was being kept but not the second.

Personally, if I am responsible for something, then I make an effort to resolve any issues. I believe this is another reason I've been able to double my salary so many times. Employers and clients like people who take ownership of problems. I do this because I want to uphold the written contract I have with my employer and go further than I need to because I want to act as a professional and I believe that professionals do more, they care more.

Perhaps this is why I'm so offended by the idea a manager would not do everything in their power to ensure an employee was paid on time. If my manager receives the results of the hard work I do but "rewards" me by failing to pay me on time, then I am offended.

There is only one way to deal with not being paid and that is to persistently and assertively remind and challenge those responsible for paying. I was able to keep reminding my manager by asking if he had signed my timesheet and expenses claim, initially doing so privately, but after he had repeatedly failed to do so, by doing so publicly at his desk. After that both the timesheet and expenses were approved. I've no desire to embarrass anyone, but there comes a point where it can be an effective method to encourage action. Had the situation continued I would have raised a formal complaint, first to my line manager, then to my agency asking for their support, and then to the client's HR and more senior line management if action did not occur immediately.

When it gets bad

Assertiveness is something I was advised to study when I was struggling in my first supervisor role. When we feel powerless there is a risk that our response will be out of proportion to the situation. Assertiveness is about understanding our rights, our responsibilities, our value, while also recognising the rights, responsibilities and value of others. Trying to understand another's point of view, listening to them, seeking resolution that allows both sides to win, empowers us and preserves our relationships.

I highly recommend the book Assertiveness at Work by Kate Back and Ken Back if you would like to study this yourself. This book taught me a lot about how to stand up for myself while also respecting others, and helped me learn how to tackle difficult situations.

There will be times when trying to resolve something without seeking advice is a mistake. If you have a mentor you can go to for advice then do so. Be careful with advice from friends. If they have been in a similar situation and were able to find a good solution, it may be worth trying what they did. However, if you have a different personality, or your work situation is different, what they tried might not work.

In some cases you may need professional or legal help. I'm a member of the British Computer Society (BCS) and my company is a member of the Federation of Small Businesses.

They, like many other professional organisations, provide a legal advice helpline free of charge (well, included in the annual subscription.)

I'm not a fan of Unions, but where they work with employees to defend their rights, they can be helpful. Being able to discuss your situation in confidence and if appropriate have a Union representative accompany you to a meeting might be exactly what you need.

It is worth saying that, in some cases, going to the organization's Human Resources (HR) department is the way to get the help you need. However, be careful, their first duty is to the company. While I believe there are many HR staff who will seek to help all employees, if you have a problem with your employer, their role and responsibility becomes blurred.

In the worst scenarios, sometimes the only right thing to do is to start looking for another job. It is always better to leave without having "burnt your bridges" but in a really bad situation perhaps that metaphor could be extended to imply a burnt bridge could act as protection from trouble chasing you across that chasm. In the heat of the moment, however, there is a real danger that saying or doing something you will later regret will have repercussions that will haunt you for years. As far as possible don't let emotion guide you.

An alternative

Doubling your salary may not be easy, but there is an alternative that can also have a transforming effect on your finances. If your income is £2,000 a month and your bills are £2,001, you are at risk of heading into debt. If you can halve your monthly bills, while maintaining your income, then you can enjoy similar benefits to doubling your salary: reduced stress along with surplus income that can be saved or used.

It is not easy to increase your income from £2,000 a month to £4,000 a month. There was a TV program in the UK some years ago, Pay Off Your Mortgage In Two Years. The premise was to see if ordinary families could effectively become debt free by fully paying off their mortgage within two years. I have to admit that I became quite disillusioned with the series as families resorted to living on porridge and forgoing all luxuries in pursuit of their goal, yet seemed unable to use this method to make sufficient progress.

It is brutally hard to deny yourself and your family all comfort for a long period of time, simply to save money. Looking at the combined family income against the debt remaining on the mortgage, it seemed clear to me that simply reducing outgoings wasn't going to be enough for any of the families to meet a two year deadline for paying off their mortgage. Instead they would have to increase their income in order to achieve that goal. I hadn't thought any of the families had managed it, but I must have either missed those episodes or forgotten because when I checked: apparently two families did indeed pay off their mortgage, by increasing their income.

There is a principle though that is vitally important to take from that show. Reducing costs does make a difference. If you double your salary from £2,000 to £4,000, but are not disciplined with your spending, you may end up with monthly bills of £4,000 and what benefit will you have gained? Sure you might be able to afford a nicer car, a better home even, but you will still be at risk of falling into debt unless you start to save.

It will be far easier to develop financial discipline if you start now, whatever your income and outgoings currently are. I admit it's tough. I don't like denying myself. It's telling then that one of the foremost charities which has for many years promoted a Real Living Wage, includes within it's projection for household expenses room for some luxuries. Yet which luxuries should be included and how many members of the family benefit from them can be a source of disagreement.

Being honest about what household income is spent on is vital. Sharing out benefits and occasional luxuries is also important to foster inclusion and value. This may mean allocating a proportion of spending to each person to do with as they wish, or could mean taking it in turn over a period of weeks to spend the money.

Is it right that a single member or group within a family spends a large proportion of income on alcohol, or cigarettes, or gambling? I don't think so. However, it may be justified that each individual is allowed an amount of money to spend as they wish with no guilt attached.

My wife and I decided a number of years ago to set aside money to spend on family fun: activities and events that the whole family could enjoy. This meant that even though I was spending a lot of time working and studying, that we would still make time, and be able to afford to do things that brought us closer together as a family. We also sought to make times for activities like board games and walks that had no financial cost.

When we've been able to, we have also budgeted to give my wife and I our own pot of free money, and to do the same for our children (though their allowances have always been far lower than ours, I have no shame in admitting that).

It's good for those who earn money and for those who stay home and work bringing up children, to be rewarded for that effort. It is also good for children to be given some measure of financial responsibility from a young age. I learned a lot from having to decide what I'd spend fifty pence on, my pocket money for a week!

We bought a tent and chose to go on camping holidays which allowed us to get a break, to rest, even though we couldn't afford to go abroad or pay for fancy hotels. It's interesting that I now hear of studies taking place that suggest spending three or more days outdoors can have a healing effect on the body: calming us, relaxing us. Even though I found different stress on some of those camping trips, frequently getting less sleep, I still always returned refreshed, with a new perspective and overall less stressed than I had been.

Are you in debt? We took out finance to enable us to "buy" a newer car. 60 monthly payments at a price we could afford. We needed a newer car and maybe had no option. The more months went by, the more I realised that the interest rate was far higher than I liked and that we were paying a lot in interest payments. Had we taken a loan out and used that to buy the car we possibly could have paid that loan off earlier and reduced the amount of interest we had to pay, but the contract I signed included penalties for early repayment. The finance company would take our money no matter what we did.

Debt can be crippling. My example above of expenses being £1 greater than income doesn't come close to describing the spiralling cost of debt when interest starts to get added to interest owed. I highly recommend the CAP Money course by Christians Against Poverty. My wife took this course and we've found it extremely helpful to use in our budgeting. We now try to avoid taking on debt and save towards buying a newer car and for all our predicted costs which will save us paying interest in the future.

If you are willing to explore more radical options, you may find it is possible to downsize, or to move to a different location that will allow you to pay less rent or have a smaller mortgage. You may be able to find another job that pays the same, but doesn't require you to pay so much to commute.

If you develop discipline now with your expenses, then when you do increase your salary, and if you continue to be disciplined, you may find you are far better off than you might have been. This has been our experience and that of many people.

The ever-shrinking hourly rate

Do you know what your hourly rate is? It's an important question to answer and you might be surprised at the many different ways to calculate it and what that implies.

Did you know that in 2017, more than forty percent of all full-time employees in the UK earned less than £20,000?

(www.ons.gov.uk/employmentandlabourmarket/peop leinwork/earningsandworkinghours/datasets/allemployeesas hetable1)

That's a large number of people, so let's take £20,000 as our starting salary to look at hourly rates. If we assume that you receive 8 public holidays each year and have 22 additional paid holidays, this leaves you working 46 weeks in the year.

Contracted full time weekly hours vary from company to company and industry to industry from 35 to 40. Let's take 37.5 hours a week as an average. That means the average employee on £20K earns £11.59 per hour. But if that's you and you're reading this book, you want to double your salary…

A lot of people think that if they work unpaid overtime, they will increase their chances of promotion and of a salary increase. Occasionally that is helpful, but look at what working an hour extra each day does to your actual hourly rate and conversely to your employer's profits:

	Mark Anderson Smith / 209	
	Contractual houly rate	Impact from unpaid overtime
Salary	£20,000	£20,000
Average holidays (in days)	30	30
Average holidays (in weeks)	6	6
Weeks worked per year (excluding holidays)	46	46
Hours worked per week	37.5	37.5
Hours extra worked a day		1
Actual hours worked each week	37.5	42.5
Hourly rate	**£11.59**	**£10.23**
Total extra hours worked annually for free		230
Annual profit to employer by working unpaid time		£2,666.67

If you consistently work an extra hour each day then your hourly rate will drop by £1.36. If you work an extra hour every working day of the year, your employer could benefit a total of £2,667 from your efforts that they don't have to pay for.

Now say you are offered a salary increase of £2,667. If you keep working that extra hour a day because you still want a salary increase next year, your hourly rate has only returned to what it was when you were working regular hours:

	Contractual houly rate	Impact from unpaid overtime	Change after salary increase
Salary	£20,000	£20,000	£22,667
Average holidays (in days)	30	30	30
Average holidays (in weeks)	6	6	6
Weeks worked per year (excluding holidays)	46	46	46
Hours worked per week	37.5	37.5	37.5
Hours extra worked a day		1	1
Actual hours worked each week	37.5	42.5	42.5
Hourly rate	**£11.59**	**£10.23**	**£11.59**
Total extra hours worked annually for free		230	230
Annual profit to employer by working unpaid time		£2,666.67	£3,022.27

Notice also that your employers benefit from you working unpaid overtime has increased. To see a real increase in your hourly rate, you would either need to stop working those extra hours or receive a higher salary increase:

	Contractual houly rate	Change after salary increase	Impact from unpaid overtime
Salary	£20,000	£22,667	£24,000
Average holidays (in days)	30	30	30
Average holidays (in weeks)	6	6	6
Weeks worked per year (excluding holidays)	46	46	46
Hours worked per week	37.5	37.5	37.5
Hours extra worked a day			1
Actual hours worked each week	37.5	37.5	42.5
Hourly rate	**£11.59**	**£13.14**	**£12.28**
Total extra hours worked annually for free			230
Annual profit to employer by working unpaid time			£3,200.00

You absolutely can increase your salary and hourly rate if your employer consistently increases your salary to both compensate you for extra hours work and adds a bonus to your bottom line base salary, but it's risky. I've worked for too many employers where that effort put in is not always rewarded.

Please understand, I'm not saying that working extra hours is a mistake, I'm simply pointing out that it is worth examining what you are being paid and contrasting that with any offer of a salary increase, or lack of offer. If you know what your contract is for, and know what extra effort you are putting in, you may be in a stronger negotiating position. Or, may be able to ask the question of whether your employer really appreciates the effort you put in.

Let's look at a more extreme example. Your base salary is £20K. Perhaps there are new clients for the firm and not enough staff to cope. You're either asked or expected to work late to make sure work is done on time. But no new staff are brought on board. Weeks go by, months and before you know it, you've been working ten-hour days and barely getting a lunch break. The value you've added to the firm for working just two hours extra each day for a year is £5,333:

	Contractual houly rate	Extreme example of unpaid overtime
Salary	£20,000	£20,000
Average holidays (in days)	30	30
Average holidays (in weeks)	6	6
Weeks worked per year (excluding holidays)	46	46
Hours worked per week	37.5	37.5
Hours extra worked a day		2
Actual hours worked each week	37.5	47.5
Hourly rate	**£11.59**	**£9.15**
Total extra hours worked annually for free		460
Annual profit to employer by working unpaid time		£5,333.33

Do you think that's extreme? It is. Yet I've worked for employers who have asked that and more from their employees. It's not so bad if you get overtime, but a more senior employee often doesn't get overtime. They're just expected to suck it up.

End of year comes round, if that employee doesn't get at least a bonus equivalent of the extra hours worked, they have lost out. But as employee friendly companies would pay overtime at time and a half, really that company should be seeking to either offer a bumper bonus, or some combination of salary increase and bonus.

Right, let's look at a more normal scenario. On a normal day you arrive at work ten minutes early and stay ten minutes late to ensure everything is tidied up. Twenty minutes extra worked each day that isn't enough to claim as overtime, but is still valuable work to an employer:

	Contractual houly rate	The impact of ten minutes
Salary	£20,000	£20,000
Average holidays (in days)	30	30
Average holidays (in weeks)	6	6
Weeks worked per year (excluding holidays)	46	46
Hours worked per week	37.5	37.5
Hours extra worked a day		0.33
Actual hours worked each week	37.5	39.15
Hourly rate	**£11.59**	**£11.11**
Total extra hours worked annually for free		75.9
Annual profit to employer by working unpaid time		£880.00

You as a worker reduced your hourly rate by 48 pence if you do this consistently and your employer doesn't have to pay you £880 a year for your extra effort. Of course, this is assuming you don't head immediately to the coffee pot, or spend that time chatting to co-workers...

Now, I'm not advocating you must turn up exactly on time and leave as soon as the clock hits the hour, I'm simply pointing out the value of our time both to us and to our employers. I advise that you do turn up before you are due to start and leave after you are due to finish. We may be contracted to work a certain number of hours, but I would rather give a bit more. That may simply allow me to justify an odd occasion where the bus or train is late, or allow me to be more relaxed as I've been able to get ahead of where my employer had a right to expect me to be. Either way, it doesn't hurt to be the person that can be counted on.

So, you've doubled your salary and now are on £40K. The same rules apply. If you have contracted hours and work extra, your new hourly rate is going to suffer:

	Contractual hourly rate	Impact from unpaid overtime
Salary	£40,000	£40,000
Average holidays (in days)	30	30
Average holidays (in weeks)	6	6
Weeks worked per year (excluding holidays)	46	46
Hours worked per week	37.5	37.5
Hours extra worked a day		1
Actual hours worked each week	37.5	42.5
Hourly rate	**£23.19**	**£20.46**
Total extra hours worked annually for free		230
Annual profit to employer by working unpaid time		£5,333.33

But the higher your base salary, the more you lose when you work unpaid hours and the more your employer gains in use of your valuable time.

These are extreme examples looking at an employee working unpaid hours over long periods of time. If there is a business need to work late or on a weekend every once in a while, don't dismiss the request out of hand unless you really cannot help. If you want to stay with your current employer and increase your salary, working the occasional late shift can be a good way of demonstrating your value to the company. But never lose sight of the fact your time is valuable and ultimately your employer should recognise that and reward you. If they don't, well, they may well lose far more than a salary increase would have cost them when you leave for an employer who actually values your time!

Saving for retirement

I was going to write in a much more positive tone about pensions in this chapter, but yesterday the papers were full of headlines about the millions that have been stolen from people after the government reformed how people can access money saved in pension schemes. On reflection, these headlines do not change what I was going to say, except to emphasize that there will always be people who are happy to steal our savings. You shouldn't assume anything about anyone when it comes to your savings. You earned that money, be careful about who you entrust it to!

I mentioned earlier that my father lost a lot of money from his private pension. Learning that made me even more wary of pensions than I was after Robert Maxwell raided the Mirror Group Pension scheme I'd been a member of. Speaking with my father recently however, he now looks back and thinks he possibly should have kept paying into his pension.

While I'm still wary of pension providers and would not want to make my retirement fully dependent on them, I can't deny that pensions are a very good idea. There are three main benefits to saving for a pension. Your overall tax burden is reduced. You hopefully will benefit from compound interest. If you are employed and working in the UK, your employer now has to match your contributions up to 3% of your annual salary, which effectively doubles your savings.

Tax is a fairly simple one. In the UK our salaries are taxed in two main ways: income tax and national insurance. If you pay into a pension, your savings come off before tax is calculated, meaning you potentially avoid tax of 32% on everything you earn above the minimum threshold, which at the time of writing is £11,500. That's an extra 32 pence in every pound you save that goes on to earn interest.

And it's the interest that really makes a difference over the forty years or so you will probably be saving for a pension. Cumulative interest benefits those who save regularly by giving you interest on the interest you've already received. It takes a while to get going, but let's look at a fairly simple example. You are twenty years old and start paying £50 each month into a pension scheme. In the first year you are not going to see much benefit:

Year 1	Pay in	Interest	Balance	Cumulative paid in	Cumulative interest
January	£50.00		£50.00	£50.00	£0.00
February	£50.00	£0.12	£100.12	£100.00	£0.12
March	£50.00	£0.25	£150.37	£150.00	£0.37
April	£50.00	£0.37	£200.74	£200.00	£0.74
May	£50.00	£0.50	£251.24	£250.00	£1.24
June	£50.00	£0.62	£301.86	£300.00	£1.86
July	£50.00	£0.74	£352.60	£350.00	£2.60
August	£50.00	£0.87	£403.47	£400.00	£3.47
September	£50.00	£1.00	£454.46	£450.00	£4.46
October	£50.00	£1.12	£505.59	£500.00	£5.59
November	£50.00	£1.25	£556.83	£550.00	£6.83
December	£50.00	£1.37	£608.21	£600.00	£8.21

A grand total of £8.32 in interest! In reality you might lose money in your first year if you have to pay start up fees. (Always read the small print! If you are an employee you should not have to pay any start up fees, but if you run your own small business, you as the employer may well pay start up fees that come out of your profits for the year.) But this is only a simple example and it's in the long term you really see the benefit. Here's what your situation looks like in year ten:

Year 10	Pay in	Interest	Balance	Cumulative paid in	Cumulative interest
January	£50.00	£15.24	£6,244.07	£5,450.00	£794.07
February	£50.00	£15.40	£6,309.47	£5,500.00	£809.47
March	£50.00	£15.56	£6,375.03	£5,550.00	£825.03
April	£50.00	£15.72	£6,440.75	£5,600.00	£840.75
May	£50.00	£15.88	£6,506.64	£5,650.00	£856.64
June	£50.00	£16.05	£6,572.68	£5,700.00	£872.68
July	£50.00	£16.21	£6,638.89	£5,750.00	£888.89
August	£50.00	£16.37	£6,705.27	£5,800.00	£905.27
September	£50.00	£16.54	£6,771.80	£5,850.00	£921.80
October	£50.00	£16.70	£6,838.50	£5,900.00	£938.50
November	£50.00	£16.87	£6,905.37	£5,950.00	£955.37
December	£50.00	£17.03	£6,972.40	£6,000.00	£972.40

You are still not earning a lot of interest each month, but in total you've now added almost £1,000 in interest to your pension while saving £6,000 yourself. Skip onto year twenty…

Year 20	Pay in	Interest	Balance	Cumulative paid in	Cumulative interest
January	£50.00	£37.68	£15,363.91	£11,450.00	£3,913.91
February	£50.00	£37.89	£15,451.80	£11,500.00	£3,951.80
March	£50.00	£38.11	£15,539.90	£11,550.00	£3,989.90
April	£50.00	£38.33	£15,628.23	£11,600.00	£4,028.23
May	£50.00	£38.54	£15,716.77	£11,650.00	£4,066.77
June	£50.00	£38.76	£15,805.54	£11,700.00	£4,105.54
July	£50.00	£38.98	£15,894.52	£11,750.00	£4,144.52
August	£50.00	£39.20	£15,983.72	£11,800.00	£4,183.72
September	£50.00	£39.42	£16,073.14	£11,850.00	£4,223.14
October	£50.00	£39.64	£16,162.78	£11,900.00	£4,262.78
November	£50.00	£39.86	£16,252.64	£11,950.00	£4,302.64
December	£50.00	£40.08	£16,342.72	£12,000.00	£4,342.72

I think that is starting to look better. Over £4,000 in interest saved and your total pension pot is now a respectable £16,415. I say respectable, but trust me, you would not want to be starting retirement with a pension less than your annual salary! Pensions are all about the long game though…

Year 30	Pay in	Interest	Balance	Cumulative paid in	Cumulative interest
January	£50.00	£67.83	£27,620.20	£17,450.00	£10,170.20
February	£50.00	£68.12	£27,738.32	£17,500.00	£10,238.32
March	£50.00	£68.41	£27,856.73	£17,550.00	£10,306.73
April	£50.00	£68.70	£27,975.44	£17,600.00	£10,375.44
May	£50.00	£68.99	£28,094.43	£17,650.00	£10,444.43
June	£50.00	£69.29	£28,213.72	£17,700.00	£10,513.72
July	£50.00	£69.58	£28,333.30	£17,750.00	£10,583.30
August	£50.00	£69.88	£28,453.18	£17,800.00	£10,653.18
September	£50.00	£70.17	£28,573.35	£17,850.00	£10,723.35
October	£50.00	£70.47	£28,693.82	£17,900.00	£10,793.82
November	£50.00	£70.77	£28,814.59	£17,950.00	£10,864.59
December	£50.00	£71.06	£28,935.65	£18,000.00	£10,935.65

By year thirty the compounding effect is starting to really show as the interest you've saved has again more than doubled to more than £11,000. And if you were to retire after working for forty years the interest received would have almost equalled what you had paid in:

Year 40	Pay in	Interest	Balance	Cumulative paid in	Cumulative interest
January	£50.00	£108.35	£44,091.65	£23,450.00	£20,641.65
February	£50.00	£108.74	£44,250.39	£23,500.00	£20,750.39
March	£50.00	£109.13	£44,409.52	£23,550.00	£20,859.52
April	£50.00	£109.53	£44,569.05	£23,600.00	£20,969.05
May	£50.00	£109.92	£44,728.97	£23,650.00	£21,078.97
June	£50.00	£110.31	£44,889.28	£23,700.00	£21,189.28
July	£50.00	£110.71	£45,049.99	£23,750.00	£21,299.99
August	£50.00	£111.11	£45,211.09	£23,800.00	£21,411.09
September	£50.00	£111.50	£45,372.60	£23,850.00	£21,522.60
October	£50.00	£111.90	£45,534.50	£23,900.00	£21,634.50
November	£50.00	£112.30	£45,696.80	£23,950.00	£21,746.80
December	£50.00	£112.70	£45,859.50	£24,000.00	£21,859.50

Now, I've used a very simple formula to work out the above numbers. Calculating interest at 3% divided by 12 to give a rough annual interest rate of 3%. In past decades pension salesmen used to assume you might receive 10%

annually, yet the reality is interest fluctuates constantly and to get higher rates you also take on higher risk which means you could lose value from your pension instead of gaining!

Fees reduce your pension pot which in turn reduces interest you can receive. However, the real killer for savers is of course inflation. If you can't receive more in interest than you are losing through inflation, you are really going to lose out. It is vital to understand the terms and conditions and to keep an eye on the progress of your pension. It's your money, take care of it!

I would hope that if you are pursuing the goal of doubling your salary that you will also make an effort to increase what you are saving. Even small but regular increases in what you put aside will have a similar effect to that of compound interest in increasing your ultimate pension pot.

If you start at age twenty paying £50 a month into your pension, and each year increase that monthly amount by just £5, so that in year two you pay £55 each month, year three £60 etc, you more than double the amount you save and earn in interest over forty years:

Year 40	Pay in	Interest	Balance	Cumulative paid in	Cumulative interest
January	£245.00	£274.52	£111,830.35	£68,105.00	£43,725.35
February	£245.00	£275.80	£112,351.15	£68,350.00	£44,001.15
March	£245.00	£277.09	£112,873.24	£68,595.00	£44,278.24
April	£245.00	£278.38	£113,396.62	£68,840.00	£44,556.62
May	£245.00	£279.67	£113,921.28	£69,085.00	£44,836.28
June	£245.00	£280.96	£114,447.24	£69,330.00	£45,117.24
July	£245.00	£282.26	£114,974.50	£69,575.00	£45,399.50
August	£245.00	£283.56	£115,503.06	£69,820.00	£45,683.06
September	£245.00	£284.86	£116,032.92	£70,065.00	£45,967.92
October	£245.00	£286.17	£116,564.09	£70,310.00	£46,254.09
November	£245.00	£287.48	£117,096.57	£70,555.00	£46,541.57
December	£245.00	£288.79	£117,630.36	£70,800.00	£46,830.36

In the last few years there is an additional benefit to taking out a pension within the UK. The government changed the law to make offering a pension compulsory to all businesses, large and small. This comes with the condition that your employer MUST match your contribution up to 3% of your annual salary. Now that's not a lot of money each month, only £50 a month for those on a £20K salary, but that is £600 a year you are getting for free. Over forty years that's £24,000 before any interest is applied! And it would double the pension pot in the first example above! If you also increase your giving, you could walk away with a healthy retirement pot.

Yet a major problem everyone on a low salary faces is that there often just isn't any spare money to save. I've faced this in my own life, yet I would argue that often there is a way to save. It might not be possible to take out a pension when your income is really low, especially if you have a family, but it should be possible to put a small amount aside each week or month. For most of my married life my wife and I did this, saving more when we could afford it, less when we couldn't, but always making an effort to put something into either a savings account, or separating it out so that the money didn't just disappear with the usual outgoings. We viewed this as short to mid-term savings, money that would only be used when something broke like the washing machine, or the kids needed new shoes urgently.

If you can get into the habit of saving in this way, that pot can slowly grow, providing a lifeline if you suddenly have a major crisis. It can also allow you to see that contributing to a pension might just be possible.

One last thought on pensions. Some people save all their life, building up their pension only to die before they receive it, or soon after. Others don't save anything and yet live a long life, scraping by with only the minimum the state gives them. Enjoy your life today as much as you are able, but do also make an effort to save.

A five and ten year plan

You remember my three goals? These were probably the closest I've ever got to writing a long term plan. I'm not the best person to give advice on long term planning. I want my future to be open to possibilities, I don't want to box myself in too much in case there is a better route I could take.

That being said, I know I could benefit from making more definite long term plans and I certainly do a lot of short and medium term planning (at least up to six months or a year.)

My three goals met some of what some people call SMART objectives:

- Specific
- Measurable
- Attainable
- Relevant
- Time restricted

Each goal was specific: to be earning £40,000 a year, to have completed a novel, to have earned a degree.

Each was measurable: I either was making progress to increasing my salary or I was not. I could tot up my word count for the day, add that to my overall word count and see how much I still had to go once I'd decided how long I wanted my novel to be. I was able to sum up the credits I gained from each course and see progress towards a degree.

It could be argued that two of these goals: to earn £40,000 a year and complete a degree by the time I was forty, were not goals I could attain. Technically I could complete the degree, but it would be at a cost to my family and indeed in the end was at a great cost. There was no way for me to know at the time how likely it would be I could achieve my goal to be earning £40,000 a year. This was more a statement of hope. Yet I would argue having achieved that goal, that I was far more likely to have succeeded in achieving it having set it as a goal than if I'd given up at the start admitting I didn't know if it was attainable.

All three goals were relevant to me: goals that would improve my life having completed them, would make my family's lives better in the long term, would fulfil dreams and aspirations I'd held most of my life.

Finally, by setting the deadline to be by the time I was forty, I gave a clear restriction on time that enabled me to focus and measure my progress towards each goal.

However, all I did at the start was write down three sentences that may have been specific, but contained no detail as to how I was going to get there.

I don't believe that matters. What I've found again and again is that the act of setting and writing down a goal is that it brings my life into sharp focus. By having multiple goals which in many ways compete for my time, I always have to make trade-offs. I'm forcing myself to project plan, a valuable skill for anyone seeking to double their salary.

Having set the goal, I commit to it. I admit that I did this in secret for my three goals. I would rather make my goals public as I've found when I do, this allows other people to decide if they also share my goals and work with me to achieve them. I would say that in setting impossible goals, it is far better to have the support of loved ones. Even the process of convincing them the goal is worth pursuing will force you to examine pitfalls and obstacles. If these are not examined and thought given to tackling them, your goal may never be completed. Eventually I did share my goals with my wife and working through concerns she had, allowed me to make better choices and allowed her to decide whether to support me or not.

I've recommended elsewhere the book: 100 ways to motivate yourself. The concept of breaking down a large task, goal or project into small easily achievable steps makes many impossible goals possible. As I understood this and applied it to my long term goals, a basic long term plan began to take shape. It was vague with only an outline of what I would need to do to achieve some of the goals, but that was enough to help me start asking more questions, which allowed me to better understand what I would need to do, which raised more questions... As I worked through the process of searching and planning and eventually seeking to do practical things in progress to the goals, each step built on the other until in hindsight, it almost became inevitable that I would achieve all three goals.

Of course there was no guarantee, but people who plan are more likely than those who do not to achieve their goals. Having a clear goal to double my salary meant that when I was offered an opportunity to get closer to that goal, I was more open to taking it, even in spite of the risks I could see. It could have gone the other way. I could have left a secure job, failed to get a contract renewal and then found myself out of work to such an extent that anyone looking at me could easily have said, you failed. Give up.

I do believe though that those who work hard, who devote themselves to learning and improving their skills are unlikely to be out of work for long.

By facing up to the risks of becoming a contractor, my wife and I saved all we could so that when I was out of work for several months and then five more full months at the end of the year, we were not made destitute. By continuing to work on my training and education, pursuing a degree, I could confidently walk into a job interview even after being out of work for five months and persuade the manager to offer me the job.

Well, I say confidently, but I was probably shaking and terrified and trying very hard to hide it.

I'm repeating myself, but setting three goals in different areas of my life had unexpected benefits. My pursuit of education helped me in my quest to increase my salary. Seeking to write a novel improved my skills in writing and research that benefited my work and studies. As I increased my salary, I was better able to afford to study and to spend time writing. I encourage you to try and set multiple complementary goals.

You don't have to know the detail of what you are going to do when you start writing a five or ten year plan, all that can be filled in later. Start with the SMART principles above as much as possible, commit to your goals, then build on them. It's worked for me, it can for you also!

Killer Inflation

I doubled my salary a third time when I reached my goal of earning £40,000 a year in 2012. Should I have relaxed, taken it easy? Even before I'd reached my target salary I'd already set a longer-term goal to be earning £100,000 a year. I don't know if I'll ever reach that goal, but I'm sure that having such a goal makes me much more likely to achieve it than if I didn't have a goal.

Did you have goals before you started reading this book? Have you set some since? If not, I encourage you to do so. If you made the effort to buy and read this book, that implies you are interested in the prospect of doubling your salary. Writing down the goal of doubling your salary and considering how you are going to achieve it could help set you on a path to earning more, but more importantly, understanding what your purpose in life is and how valuable you are.

If you don't make an effort to improve your lot, then you at least need to be aware of the consequences. Remember my crazy notion that I wanted to be earning at least £1,000 for each year of my life? I had that thought back in 1990. If I had achieved it then, but done nothing to continue to increase my earnings, I would have found my earnings buying me less and less each year. By quite a substantial amount:

Year	The magic number	Inflation rate	Reduction in value
1990	£1,000	3%	£30
1991	£970	3%	£29
1992	£941	3%	£28
1993	£913	3%	£27
1994	£885	3%	£27
1995	£859	3%	£26
1996	£833	3%	£25
1997	£808	3%	£24
1998	£784	3%	£24
1999	£760	3%	£23
2000	£737	3%	£22
2001	£715	3%	£21
2002	£694	3%	£21
2003	£673	3%	£20
2004	£653	3%	£20
2005	£633	3%	£19
2006	£614	3%	£18
2007	£596	3%	£18
2008	£578	3%	£17
2009	£561	3%	£17
2010	£544	3%	£16
2011	£527	3%	£16
2012	£512	3%	£15
2013	£496	3%	£15
2014	£481	3%	£14
2015	£467	3%	£14
2016	£453	3%	£14
2017	£439	3%	£13
2018	£426	3%	£13

In the twenty-eight years since, inflation would have robbed me of almost 60% of the value of my earnings!

Just to stand still in terms of my earnings paying the same level of bills etc, I would have had to increase my earnings like so:

Year	The magic number	Inflation rate	Increase in value
1990	£1,000	3%	£30
1991	£1,030	3%	£31
1992	£1,061	3%	£32
1993	£1,093	3%	£33
1994	£1,126	3%	£34
1995	£1,159	3%	£35
1996	£1,194	3%	£36
1997	£1,230	3%	£37
1998	£1,267	3%	£38
1999	£1,305	3%	£39
2000	£1,344	3%	£40
2001	£1,384	3%	£42
2002	£1,426	3%	£43
2003	£1,469	3%	£44
2004	£1,513	3%	£45
2005	£1,558	3%	£47
2006	£1,605	3%	£48
2007	£1,653	3%	£50
2008	£1,702	3%	£51
2009	£1,754	3%	£53
2010	£1,806	3%	£54
2011	£1,860	3%	£56
2012	£1,916	3%	£57
2013	£1,974	3%	£59
2014	£2,033	3%	£61
2015	£2,094	3%	£63
2016	£2,157	3%	£65
2017	£2,221	3%	£67
2018	£2,288	3%	£69

If I hadn't more than doubled my salary in those twenty-eight years I'd have been going backwards.

Do you understand why it's important to have a plan in place to double your salary? If you don't you are at the mercy of inflation and whoever is paying your salary.

A final word

A young child stands in a puddle, rain splashing water up onto bare legs above wellington boots. The child is bawling his eyes out. "I can't move! I'm stuck!"

How long will that child stand there? Until they are picked up and carried away? Until a parent takes their hand and pulls them along? Or will they eventually, perhaps even slowly and resentfully, pick up one muddy boot and start walking out of the puddle?

You are not a child.

You may however be stuck in a job that does not value your skills and potential. Debt may have you trapped, every month stealing a little more of your income, robbing you of your peace. You might be frustrated with no hope things can change.

You are not a child.

Perhaps you think all this is beyond you. If you are in a job then possibly the risk of change seems too much, even if you stand little chance of promotion or salary increase.

You are not a child, though you were one once. As was I…

I think I was eight when my sister and I went to stay with a friend who lived in Mossbank in Shetland. We all went down to the beach, a sandy V shaped beach that stretched out and expanded as the tide went out to what seemed to my young eyes like half a mile. We spent a good couple of hours playing on the sand and in the shallow pools of water that had been left behind. All was well until we realised the tide had come in around us, leaving us trapped on a bank of sand slightly higher than the rising water.

I was wearing new shoes and was under strict instructions not to get them in the salt water. Yet there was no way to get to shore without wading through the water. We were trapped. All the time we stood there, the water kept rising, the sand bank we were stood on became narrower. I was in tears knowing I would get in trouble for wrecking my new shoes.

I don't know who came up with the idea. Our friend, my sister, me... It could have been any one of us. The water wasn't deep. All we had to do was take off our shoes and socks and walk to shore. And so we did.

I was trapped, but only because I didn't know there was a way out. There is always a way out.

You are an adult, not a child.

You have options available to you whether you realise them or not. Sometimes the way we deal with situations seems little different to how a child would act. I spent a long decade telling myself I didn't need to go to college or university. I know that not everyone does, but for me, eventually, I had to take that route.

That child, stuck in a puddle, I think that was me. I have a vague memory of being caught in the rain, probably only wearing shorts and a t-shirt and for some reason those wellington boots. Maybe I was exhausted from a long walk. Maybe I was angry that my parents wouldn't do what I wanted. I guess it doesn't matter why any of us are stuck where we are. Even as adults, sometimes all we need to do to get unstuck is take one and then another baby step forwards.

If this book resonates with you, if you feel that doubling your salary could make a real difference to your life, and it all seems impossible, too risky, then know this: to pursue such an ambition as doubling your salary is risky, but to leave yourself at the mercy of others is even riskier. The first steps you can take are all without risk:

- Deciding if you are in the right career
- Working out whether there is opportunity for you to earn more in your preferred career
- Looking into relevant training or educational courses

Without spending a pound, you can investigate your options and open your mind to the possibility of change. Simply looking at your options and working out whether that can have a positive impact on your finances can help take away some of the fear of change.

If you are comfortable or at least open to the idea of doubling your salary, then I would encourage you to start to ask: "Why would any client or employer pay me what I want to earn? Can I provide a service that gives them greater value than the cost of paying me?" The answer to the first question comes from answering the second. If you can now start to develop the mindset that wherever you work and for whomever you work you intend to provide greater value than you cost to be employed, you allow yourself to start questioning yourself as to whether you are actually doing this.

If you can learn to analyse your own work and justify your value to your employer, you are developing a valuable skill that allows you to show how much you are worth. And you are worth far more than you realise!

I'm still on the same journey, trying once again to double my salary. I'm earning more than I ever have before and I'm conscious of the question: how much will be enough?

I think that's the wrong question. I've had employers and clients ask me a similar question when I tell them I'm leaving. The fact is that I don't ever want money to be my sole motivator.

Yet I know that money can be a helpful tool and so while I'm able to earn it I will. There are many things I feel I need to do with the money I earn.

I only recently started saving into a pension again. I've a long way to go before my pension pot will approach anything like enough to support me and my wife in retirement. If I can earn more, I will save more.

I had this crazy idea that I would like to pay for my kids to go through university. For someone who couldn't afford to save into a pension at the time that was a crazy idea, even if the motive behind it was good. Now, on reflection, I'm not sure that was such a good idea. I succeeded in education because I wanted and needed to learn. I succeeded because I paid my way (through most of it) and knew how much it was costing me. I'm not sure that it is helpful to take that away from my kids.

That being said, I still want to be able to throw a celebration when they get married. I'd like to be able to help them put together a deposit for a new home.

I would also like to be free from debt. Completely free: no mortgage sucking the lifeblood out of my income each month. No outstanding loans. That would be a good place to be and I would rather work my way out of debt sooner than later.

I would like to see more of this amazing world we live in. I've been blessed to walk on three continents over the last thirty years. I've been as far from East to West as Beijing and Washington DC. I have a childhood ambition to see the Grand Canyon and would love to see Central America and New Zealand. Travel like that ain't cheap, but maybe doesn't require too much more money than I'm currently earning if I save more.

My current target for annual income is £100,000 a year. That was Goal 78 of my 100 goals: Be earning £100,000 a year within 5 years. I didn't make it! But that number is an interesting one. I don't really care if I do earn £100,000 a year. Instead, what I'm much more interested in is the flexibility that having a high daily rate offers. If I can reach the point where I'm earning £50,000 over the course of a six-month contract, I can afford to be without work six months of the year. Six months when I can write, spend time with my family, perhaps explore some of my other interests.

I've already made progress towards that aim. In the last five years I've had a couple where I've managed to take almost the whole school summer holidays off. Something I would never have been able to do in a permanent job. Is that something you would like to be able to do?

I can imagine critics saying: it's just not possible for everyone to double their salary!

But what if it is?

What if everyone started working harder? What if we all discovered our purpose in life? What if we all sought to better ourselves? What could we make of this world if we all really tried?

The argument might go: but there's no more money in the world.

Except, ten years ago we didn't have this much money in the world as exists today. Twenty years ago, there was less money still. The fact is that we are creating money all the time because money is just a tool that we invented to make buying and selling easier and the only restriction on how much of it exists is what we decide.

The response could be: but if we all have more money it will be worth less, so how do we benefit?

If money is worth less, the rich stand to lose far more than the poor, if the reason money is worth less is because the poor have doubled their salary would that really be a bad thing?

Objections are raised: it was easy for you, it won't be for me.

No, it wasn't easy for me. It was hard work over many years. I gave up time with my family (and am still not sure that was worth it), and time when I needed rest. I forced myself to study and work harder. I made every effort to learn. It won't be easy for you either. But it is possible.

I cannot end this book without reminding you of a couple of statements Jesus made about money and wealth. He said the love of money is a root of all kinds of evil, and asked: what good it does for a man to gain the whole world but lose their soul.

Neither of these statements should discourage you from trying to free yourself from poverty. I have found though that the pursuit of wealth has led me down some dark paths. Be careful what priorities you set and the goals you aim for. I hold to another statement of Jesus, that we should seek God first and he will provide for our needs. I believe that it is as I've done this that I've seen real beneficial change in my life.

I hope this book has inspired you and will encourage you to improve your life. I would love to hear from you and there are contact details at the end of this book. Do let me know how you're getting on.

I wrote earlier and want to finish up by reminding you:

You are an incredible human being, created in the image of an incredible and awesome God. Each of us can do amazing things if we will only believe and persevere.

If you take on the challenge to attempt to double your salary, may you do so without losing your soul.

Final prompts and suggestions

Have you researched how much people can earn in your ideal career?

Who do you have (or have had) as role models in your life?

What obstacles do you feel that you face right now?

What could you do to overcome these?

Are you more attracted to a pyramid or wigwam type company?

Are you working on the foundations of who you are, your character, your work ethic, how you present yourself, and your skills and knowledge?

Are you using the privilege and advantages you have, while also seeking to expand on these?

What is your ideal career?

Carry out an analysis of what you enjoy doing, what you are skilled at, and what other people compliment you for.

Use online jobsites to identify the skills and experience you will need to secure your ideal role, then use that knowledge to determine the training you take and stepping-stone jobs you take.

Are you willing to commit to long term effort to learn and train to develop a professional career and keep up to date with the latest best practice and technology?

Have you explored whether there may be free training or courses available, or if bursaries and grants might be open to you?

Make notes after every interview, what went well, what you could have said or done differently, what you should avoid saying in future.

Are you comfortable in what you wear to interviews? Are you presenting a professional image?

Have you sought out feedback on your CV?

How can you reduce your current expenses to allow you to save more now?

Have you worked out what you are actually paid for the hours you work?

Are you saving for your retirement?

Write out a five and ten year plan for your career.

Do you understand the impact inflation will have on your salary over the long term?

Have you considered how much time you are willing to devote to improving yourself bearing in mind family commitments?

Are you willing to risk leaving a secure but lowly paid job to gain new skills that will help you in the long term?

Are you willing to examine yourself, to ask others how they perceive you and develop new habits that will enable you to succeed?

Why would any client or employer pay you what you want to earn?

Can you provide them with a service that gives them greater value than the cost of paying you?

Author's note and appreciation

Thank you for reading Double Your Salary! Please rate and review this book on www.goodreads.com, or if you bought through an online store, on their site. Even a short sentence is helpful to let other people know what you thought of the book.

If you would like to sign up to my mailing list you can do so at: www.dragonlake.co.uk

I would love to hear if this book has been helpful to you. You can contact me through:

Email: mark@dragonlake.co.uk
LinkedIn: www.linkedin.com/in/marksqlsmith/
Facebook: www.facebook.com/my100goals/
Twitter: @my100goals

This book has been part of my journey and neither the book nor the experiences I've been able to share in it would have been possible without the support of many people.

Firstly my wife and children who have been a constant encouragement and support and have given me much to be thankful for.

I've dedicated this book to my parents. They never let my childhood fantasies go to my head, but at the same time encouraged me to believe anything was possible.

There have been many employers and managers who have given me a chance to prove myself, also colleagues and mentors who have given guidance and shared their knowledge. Without them, this book could not have been written. A few names stand out: Jimmy Balfour, Jack Leslie, Reidar and Astrid Vetvik, Rev Ian Thomson, Michael Davis, Richard Hind, Alex Winton, Andrew Tait, Scott Wilson,

Peter Grant, Charlie Harris, Fraser Graham, Alastair Sandilands, Paul Boyle and my good friend Dan King who advised me to learn SQL. There are many others. I am grateful to you all.

There have also been several people who have read early drafts of this book and given useful feedback, some of whom such as John Barton and Alex Winton who went above and beyond. A huge thank you to them and to: David Logue, Louise Logue, Aidan Henderson, Robert Taggart, Peter Leonard, David Ampofo, Trudy Richardson, Margaret Muir, Tom Muir, Dan King, Grace Welsh, Caroline Johnston, Robert Maxwell, Sharon Russell, Alan Welsh, Dawn Smith, William White, Vincent Brennan, Michael Davis and Jack Redmond.

Any issues remaining with the book are fully my responsibility.

Finally I want to thank the church families that have been such a rich blessing to us as a family on our journey. Hillingdon Park Baptist Church supported us when we might have become homeless, then while in Tajikistan. York Elim supported us while in Tajikistan and were there for us when we returned. Cornerstone Christian Fellowship welcomed us on our move to Scotland. There have also been many others from churches around the country who have blessed us, supported us, taught us and shared with us.

If you enjoyed this book, you may like to try one of my two novels which are available in print and ebook format:

Fallen Warriors

In the city of York, a young nurse dies in a tragic accident but is mysteriously brought back to life. As she attempts to find out and understand what happened, a group of ordinary people find themselves drawn together: a homeless man tormented by his past, a thief who has crossed a dangerous line, a young Muslim girl searching for answers, a detective hiding a secret, a woman who wants to remove the pastor of her church. Unknown to any of them, an Islamic group secretly plots to form a new Caliphate in the centre of England. York becomes the battle ground for the largest terrorist attack ever faced in the West. Fallen warriors are called to stand and fight, but will they stand or will they fall?

The Great Scottish Land Grab

When his wife is threatened while on a walking holiday in the Scottish Highlands, Robert Castle tries to get justice, only to find the people of Scotland have little rights on their historic land.

Meanwhile, Scotland is preparing to vote on independence when the deaths of senior members of the Scottish Government forces an election.

Disillusioned by his research into Scotland's history, and sensing that the theft of Scotland's land over many centuries has robbed the people of their opportunity to be independent, Castle establishes a new political party and fights for a modern day land grab - to reverse the clearances and return the land that was stolen from Scotland's people.

Challenging an out of touch parliament, Robert turns government on its head by introducing Cafe Politics - a way for communities to debate and agree their own policies.

But how far will Robert go in his determination to overturn the injustice of the Highland Clearances and will he lead Scotland to a better future or into civil war?

Recommended Reading

There are a number of books that have helped me in my career, many of which are quite technical and only useful for specific job roles. The following selection of books are recommended as I believe they will be widely useful. There are some technical books in this short list, but these may still be helpful to anyone who is interested in using software to simplify their job and to automate computer processes.

100 Ways To Motivate Yourself – Steve Chandler
Assertiveness at Work – Kate Back and Ken Back
Goals! – Brian Tracy
Holy Bible – Various
Managing for Dummies – Bob Nelson and Peter Economy
Mastering Microsoft Access 2000 Development – Alison Balter
(There is a more recent edition)
Nevertheless – John Kirkby
Rain: What a Paperboy Learned About Business – Jeffrey J. Fox
Use Your Head – Tony Buzan
VBA and Macros for Microsoft Excel – Bill Jelen and Tracy Syrstad

Index

A

B

C

K

L

M

N

O
obstacles 131-141, 153, 225
overtime 208-216

P
panic attack 53
pension 31, 32-34, 217-223, 236
  a long life 223
  compounding 220-221
  cumulative interest 218-221
  match contributions 217
  pot 219-222
permanent employee 123, 178, 199
pitfalls and obstacles 225
plan 73, 139
  business 63
  five year/ten year 48-49, 224-227
  long term 224
possibility of change 235
powerless 202
presentable 144-145
priorities 103, 150, 196-197
privilege 152-153
productivity 48, 91
professionalism 151, 187
project plan 81, 225
promotion 28, 150, 199, 208
prompts and suggestions 19, 39, 68, 96, 127, 239
purpose in life 7, 228, 237
pyramid organisation 142-143

R
references 150, 193
relevant (goals) 224-225
responsibility 194-195, 197-198, 201

About the author

Mark Anderson Smith is Director of Goal 31 Ltd, a successful small consulting business operating in the central belt of Scotland, where he lives with his wife and children. He has developed business applications for the Crown Prosecution Service, Barclays, Prudential, Sky, and the BBC; simplifying processes, making data easier to use, and saving his clients money.

Doubling his salary three times over twenty five years, Mark believes that many people could do the same if they were aware of the possibility and willing to commit to the goal.

He is the author of two novels: Fallen Warriors and The Great Scottish Land Grab, this is his first non-fiction book.

Mark is passionate about goals, having seen what a dramatic effect it can have when goals are set that build on each other. A few years ago he accepted a challenge to write down 100 goals. To date he still hasn't stood on a new planet or learned to fly, but insists there is still time…

Lightning Source UK Ltd.
Milton Keynes UK
UKHW041454110719
345940UK00001B/50/P